THE CHRYSOSTOM BIBLE
A Commentary Series for Preaching and Teaching
Hebrews: A Commentary

THE CHRYSOSTOM BIBLE
A Commentary Series for Preaching and Teaching

Hebrews: A Commentary

Paul Nadim Tarazi

OCABS PRESS
ST PAUL, MINNESOTA 55124
2014

THE CHRYSOSTOM BIBLE
HEBREWS: A COMMENTARY

Copyright © 2014 by
Paul Nadim Tarazi

ISBN 1-60191-025-8

All rights reserved.

PRINTED IN THE UNITED STATES OF AMERICA

Other Books by the Author

I Thessalonians: A Commentary
Galatians: A Commentary

The Old Testament: An Introduction

Volume 1: Historical Traditions, revised edition
Volume 2: Prophetic Traditions
Volume 3: Psalms and Wisdom

The New Testament: An Introduction

Volume 1: Paul and Mark
Volume 2: Luke and Acts
Volume 3: Johannine Writings
Volume 4: Matthew and the Canon

The Chrysostom Bible

Genesis: A Commentary
Philippians: A Commentary
Romans: A Commentary
Colossians & Philemon: A Commentary
1 Corinthians: A Commentary
Ezekiel: A Commentary
Joshua: A Commentary
2 Corinthians: A Commentary
Isaiah: A Commentary
Jeremiah: A Commentary

Land and Covenant

The Chrysostom Bible
Hebrews: A Commentary

Copyright © 2014 by Paul Nadim Tarazi
All rights reserved.

ISBN 1-60191-025-8

Published by OCABS Press, St. Paul, Minnesota.
Printed in the United States of America.

Books are available through OCABS Press at special discounts for bulk purchases in the United States by academic institutions, churches, and other organizations. For more information please email OCABS Press at press@ocabs.org.

Abbreviations

Books by the Author

1 Thess *I Thessalonians: A Commentary,* Crestwood, NY: St. Vladimir's Seminary Press, 1982

Gal *Galatians: A Commentary,* Crestwood, NY: St. Vladimir's Seminary Press, 1994

OTI₁ *The Old Testament: An Introduction, Volume 1: Historical Traditions,* revised edition, Crestwood, NY: St. Vladimir's Seminary Press, 2003

OTI₂ *The Old Testament: An Introduction, Volume 2: Prophetic Traditions,* Crestwood, NY: St. Vladimir's Seminary Press, 1994

OTI₃ *The Old Testament: An Introduction, Volume 3: Psalms and Wisdom,* Crestwood, NY: St. Vladimir's Seminary Press, 1996

NTI₁ *The New Testament: An Introduction, Volume 1: Paul and Mark,* Crestwood, NY: St. Vladimir's Seminary Press, 1999

NTI₂ *The New Testament: An Introduction, Volume 2: Luke and Acts,* Crestwood, NY: St. Vladimir's Seminary Press, 2001

NTI₃ *The New Testament: An Introduction, Volume 3: Johannine Writings,* Crestwood, NY: St. Vladimir's Seminary Press, 2004

NTI₄ *The New Testament: An Introduction, Volume 4: Matthew and the Canon,* St. Paul, MN: OCABS Press, 2009

C-Gen *Genesis: A Commentary.* The Chrysostom Bible. St. Paul, MN: OCABS Press, 2009

C-Phil *Philippians: A Commentary.* The Chrysostom Bible. St. Paul, MN: OCABS Press, 2009

C-Rom *Romans: A Commentary.* The Chrysostom Bible. St. Paul, MN: OCABS Press, 2010

C-Col *Colossians & Philemon: A Commentary.* The Chrysostom Bible. St. Paul, MN: OCABS Press, 2010

C-1Cor *1 Corinthians: A Commentary.* The Chrysostom Bible. St. Paul, MN: OCABS Press, 2011

C-Ezek *Ezekiel: A Commentary.* The Chrysostom Bible. St. Paul, MN: OCABS Press, 2012

C-Josh	*Joshua: A Commentary.* The Chrysostom Bible. St. Paul, MN: OCABS Press, 2013
C-2Cor	*2 Corinthians: A Commentary.* The Chrysostom Bible. St. Paul, MN: OCABS Press, 2013
C-Is	*Isaiah: A Commentary.* The Chrysostom Bible. St. Paul, MN: OCABS Press, 2013
C-Jer	*Jeremiah: A Commentary.* The Chrysostom Bible. St. Paul, MN: OCABS Press, 2013
LAC	*Land and Covenant,* St. Paul, MN: OCABS Press, 2009

Abbreviations

Books of the Old Testament*

Gen	Genesis	Job	Job	Hab		Habakkuk
Ex	Exodus	Ps	Psalms	Zeph		Zephaniah
Lev	Leviticus	Prov	Proverbs	Hag		Haggai
Num	Numbers	Eccl	Ecclesiastes	Zech		Zechariah
Deut	Deuteronomy	Song	Song of Solomon	Mal		Malachi
Josh	Joshua	Is	Isaiah	Tob		Tobit
Judg	Judges	Jer	Jeremiah	Jdt		Judith
Ruth	Ruth	Lam	Lamentations	Wis		Wisdom
1 Sam	1 Samuel	Ezek	Ezekiel	Sir	Sirach	(Ecclesiasticus)
2 Sam	2 Samuel	Dan	Daniel	Bar		Baruch
1 Kg	1 Kings	Hos	Hosea	1 Esd		1 Esdras
2 Kg	2 Kings	Joel	Joel	2 Esd		2 Esdras
1 Chr	1 Chronicles	Am	Amos	1 Macc		1 Maccabees
2 Chr	2 Chronicles	Ob	Obadiah	2 Macc		2 Maccabees
Ezra	Ezra	Jon	Jonah	3 Macc		3 Maccabees
Neh	Nehemiah	Mic	Micah	4 Macc		4 Maccabees
Esth	Esther	Nah	Nahum			

Books of the New Testament

Mt	Matthew	Eph	Ephesians	Heb	Hebrews
Mk	Mark	Phil	Philippians	Jas	James
Lk	Luke	Col	Colossians	1 Pet	1 Peter
Jn	John	1 Thess	1 Thessalonians	2 Pet	2 Peter
Acts	Acts	2 Thess	2 Thessalonians	1 Jn	1 John
Rom	Romans	1 Tim	1 Timothy	2 Jn	2 John
1 Cor	1 Corinthians	2 Tim	2 Timothy	3 Jn	3 John
2 Cor	2 Corinthians	Titus	Titus	Jude	Jude
Gal	Galatians	Philem	Philemon	Rev	Revelation

*Following the larger canon known as the Septuagint.

Contents

Preface	*15*
Introduction	*19*
Chapter 1	*23*
Vv. 1-4	*23*
Vv. 5-14	*31*
Chapter 2	*41*
Vv. 1-4	*41*
Vv. 5-18	*42*
Chapter 3	*53*
Vv. 1-6	*53*
Vv. 7-19	*60*
Chapter 4	*65*
Vv. 1-13	*65*
Chapter 5	*81*
Vv. 4:14-16	*81*
Vv. 5:1-10	*83*
Chapter 6	*87*
Vv. 5:11-14	*87*
Vv. 6:1-12	*87*
Vv. 13-20	*94*
Chapter 7	*97*
Vv. 7:1-28	*97*

Chapter 8	*111*
Vv. 8:1-13	111
Chapter 9	*119*
Vv. 9:1-28	119
Chapter 10	*131*
Vv. 10:1-39	131
Chapter 11	*139*
Vv. 11:1-40	139
Chapter 12	*149*
Vv. 12:1-29	149
Chapter 13	*157*
Vv. 13:1-25	157
Further Reading	*169*
Commentaries and Studies	*169*
Articles	*170*

Preface

The present Bible Commentary Series is not so much in honor of John Chrysostom as it is to continue and promote his legacy as an interpreter of the biblical texts for preaching and teaching God's congregation, in order to prod its members to proceed on the way they started when they accepted God's calling. Chrysostom's virtual uniqueness is that he did not subscribe to any hermeneutic or methodology, since this would amount to introducing an extra-textual authority over the biblical texts. For him, scripture is its own interpreter. Listening to the texts time and again allowed him to realize that "call" and "read (aloud)" are not interconnected realities; rather, they are one reality since they both are renditions of the same Hebrew verb *qara'*. Given that words read aloud are words of instruction for one "to do them," the only valid reaction would be to hear, listen, obey, and abide by these words. All these connotations are subsumed in the same Hebrew verb *šamaʻ*. On the other hand, these scriptural "words of life" are presented as readily understandable utterances of a father to his children (Isaiah 1:2-3). The recipients are never asked to engage in an intellectual debate with their divine instructor, or even among themselves, to fathom what he is saying. The Apostle to the Gentiles followed in the footsteps of the Prophets to Israel by handing down to them the Gospel, that is, the Law of God's Spirit through his Christ (Romans 8:2; Galatians 6:2) as fatherly instruction (1 Corinthians 4:15). He in turn wrote readily understandable letters to be read aloud. It is in these same footsteps that Chrysostom followed, having learned from both the Prophets and Paul that the same "words of life" carry also the sentence of death at the hand of the scriptural God, Judge of all

(Deuteronomy 28; Joshua 8:32-35; Psalm 82; Matthew 3:4-12; Romans 2:12-16; 1 Corinthians 10:1-11; Revelation 20:11-15).

While theological debates and hermeneutical theories come and go after having fed their proponents and their fans with passing human glory, the Golden Mouth's expository homilies, through the centuries, fed and still feed myriads of believers in so many traditions and countries. Virtually banned from dogmatic treatises, he survives in the hearts of "those who have ears to hear." His success is due to his commitment to exegesis rather than to futile hermeneutics. The latter behaves as someone who dictates on a living organism what it is supposed to be, whereas exegesis submits to that organism and endeavors to decipher it through trial and error. There is as much a far cry between the text and the theories about it as there is between a living organism and the theories about it. The biblical texts are the reality of God imparted through their being read aloud in the midst of the congregation, disregarding the value of the sermon that follows. The sermon, much less a theological treatise, is at best an invitation to hear and obey the text. Assessing the shape of an invitation card has no value whatsoever when it comes to the dinner itself; the guests are fed by the dinner, not by the invitation or its phrasing (Luke 14:16-24; Matthew 22:1-14).

This commentary series does not intend to promote Chrysostom's ideas as a public relation manager would do, but rather to follow in the footsteps of his approach as true children and heirs are expected to do. He used all the contemporary tools at his disposal to communicate God's written instruction to his hearers, as a doctor would with his patients, without spending unnecessary energy on peripheral debates requiring the use of professional jargon incomprehensible to the commoner. The writers of this series will try to do the same: muster to the best of their ability all necessary contemporary knowledge to communicate to the general readers the biblical message without burdening them with data unnecessary for that purpose. Whenever it will be deemed necessary or even helpful to do so, and in order to curtail burdensome and lengthy technical asides within the commentaries, specialized monographs related either to specific topics or to the scriptural background—literary, socio-political, or archeological—will be issued as companions to the series.

Paul Nadim Tarazi
Editor

Introduction

In his earliest letter, Galatians, which served as a blue print for all his subsequent correspondence, Paul committed to writ his gospel of the one community of Jews and Gentiles around the one table fellowship (Gal 2:1-14). It is thus only befitting that his school bracketed his literary corpus of fourteen epistles between two magisterial letters—Romans, addressed to the residents of the capital of the Gentile Roman empire, and Hebrews, addressed to the Jews who were still dreaming of the restoration of the earthly Jerusalem that was destroyed by the Romans. The focus of Galatians is that legal (law-ful) righteousness, which is the concern par excellence of Rome, does not proceed from that city, but rather it is granted by the scriptural God who, as judge of all, resides in *his* city, a topic that is developed in Romans. However, God's city is not, as it was assumed by the Jews, the earthly Jerusalem that lay subjugated by Rome, but rather the "Jerusalem above" (Gal 4:26), the heavenly city of Zion, toward which the believers are heading. This topic forms the main focus of Hebrews:

> By faith Abraham obeyed when he was called to go out to a place which he was to receive as an inheritance; and he went out, not knowing where he was to go. By faith he sojourned in the land of promise, as in a foreign land, living in tents with Isaac and Jacob, heirs with him of the same promise. For he looked forward to the city which has foundations, whose builder and maker is God. (11:8-10)
>
> These all died in faith, not having received what was promised, but having seen it and greeted it from afar, and having acknowledged that they were strangers and exiles on the earth. For people who speak thus make it clear that they are seeking a

homeland. If they had been thinking of that land from which they had gone out, they would have had opportunity to return. But as it is, they desire a better country, that is, a heavenly one. Therefore God is not ashamed to be called their God, for he has prepared for them a city. (11:13-16)

But you have come to Mount Zion and to the city of the living God, the heavenly Jerusalem, and to innumerable angels in festal gathering, and to the assembly of the first-born who are enrolled in heaven, and to a judge who is God of all, and to the spirits of just men made perfect, and to Jesus, the mediator of a new covenant, and to the sprinkled blood that speaks more graciously than the blood of Abel. (12:22-24)

For here we have no lasting city, but we seek the city which is to come. (13:14)

In scripture, the main facet of Jerusalem, as the city of God, is the temple and its service as witnessed in 1 Kings 5-8 and 1 Chronicles 21-29 where the king, God's anointed, functions also a high priest. The centrality of temple service for the life of the city remains valid even in the heavenly Zion where offerings are presented to God and songs of praises are raised in his honor, as is evident in the last two parts (Books IV [Ps 90-106] and V [Ps 107-150]) of the Book of Psalms. This explains why the author of Hebrews is so keen to underscore the function of Jesus, the eschatological messenger and Christ (Anointed) of God, as also high priest. This theme not only brackets the epistle (Heb 2:17; 13:11), but is also a crimson thread that runs through its entirety (3:1; 4:14, 15; 5:1, 5, 6, 10; 6:20; 7:1, 3, 11, 15, 16, 17, 21, 26; 8:1, 3, 4; 9:7, 11, 25; 10:11, 21). In the absence of the physical city and temple of Jerusalem, the Jews are invited to join the Gentiles, their brethren and commensals in the gospel, "to present your bodies as a living sacrifice, holy and acceptable to God, which is your spiritual worship" (Rom 12:1).

Chapter 1

Vv. 1-4 *¹Πολυμερῶς καὶ πολυτρόπως πάλαι ὁ θεὸς λαλήσας τοῖς πατράσιν ἐν τοῖς προφήταις ² ἐπ᾽ ἐσχάτου τῶν ἡμερῶν τούτων ἐλάλησεν ἡμῖν ἐν υἱῷ, ὃν ἔθηκεν κληρονόμον πάντων, δι᾽ οὗ καὶ ἐποίησεν τοὺς αἰῶνας· ³ὃς ὢν ἀπαύγασμα τῆς δόξης καὶ χαρακτὴρ τῆς ὑποστάσεως αὐτοῦ, φέρων τε τὰ πάντα τῷ ῥήματι τῆς δυνάμεως αὐτοῦ, καθαρισμὸν τῶν ἁμαρτιῶν ποιησάμενος ἐκάθισεν ἐν δεξιᾷ τῆς μεγαλωσύνης ἐν ὑψηλοῖς, ⁴τοσούτῳ κρείττων γενόμενος τῶν ἀγγέλων ὅσῳ διαφορώτερον παρ᾽ αὐτοὺς κεκληρονόμηκεν ὄνομα.*

¹In many and various ways God spoke of old to our fathers by the prophets; ²but in these last days he has spoken to us by a Son, whom he appointed the heir of all things, through whom also he created the world. ³He reflects the glory of God and bears the very stamp of his nature, upholding the universe by his word of power. When he had made purification for sins, he sat down at the right hand of the Majesty on high, ⁴having become as much superior to angels as the name he has obtained is more excellent than theirs.

The prologue to the Book of Hebrews is one of scripture's most magisterial passages. Despite its succinctness—a mere four verses—it presents as well as presages the entire thesis of the study: the Christ of the Pauline gospel is the end point—"in these last days"—of the Old Testament trajectory that started with the Law: "For Christ is the end (*telos*; end point, aim, target) of the law, that every one who has faith may be justified." (Rom 10:4) As will become clear in the body of the letter, the key thought that brackets its entirety is "heritage," that is, the heritage in the place of "rest" (Heb 3:11, 18; 4:1, 3, 5, 8-11), promised by God to the fathers, a promise that will encompass the nations as well as Israel, as taught in the Latter Prophets.[1]

The opening statement that covers 1:1-2 is, in a nutshell, the message of the parable of the tenants of the vineyard,[2] which is the concluding parable in Mark and thus wraps up that Gospel's parabolic teaching.[3] After a long series of "servants" (Mk 12:3-5), the last emissary sent is the "beloved son" (v.6), the "heir" who is the recipient of the "inheritance" (v.7).[4] This teaching reflects Paul's statement in Galatians that, after a series of "guardians and trustees," the heir is sent, at the "date set by the father," and he will include Gentiles as well as Jews in the "inheritance." This teaching is also revisited in Romans:

> I mean that the heir, as long as he is a child, is no better than a slave, though he is the owner of all the estate (*kyrios pantōn*; lord of all and everything);[5] but he is under guardians and trustees until the *date set* (*prothesmias* [from the same root as *ethēken*]; time appointed [KJV]) by the father. So with us; when we were children, we were slaves to the elemental spirits of the universe. But when the time had fully come, God sent forth his Son, born of woman, born under the law, to redeem those who were under the law, so that we might receive adoption as sons. And because you are sons, God has sent the Spirit of his Son into our hearts, crying, "Abba! Father!" So through God you are no longer a slave but a son, and if a son then an heir. (Gal 4:1-7)

---

[1] See especially Is 2:2-4; 42:6-7; 49:5-6; 66:15-21; Jer 3:17-19; 16:19.
[2] Mk 12:1-12; Lk 20:9-19; Mt 21:33-46.
[3] "And they tried to arrest him, but feared the multitude, for they perceived that he had told the parable against them; so they left him and went away." (Mk 12:12)
[4] The original for "has obtained" in RSV's Heb 1:4 is *keklēronomēken* (has inherited).
[5] Compare with *klēronomon pantōn* (heir of all things), the position in which the "son" is appointed (*ethēken*; Heb 1:2).

For you did not receive the spirit of slavery to fall back into fear, but you have received the spirit of sonship. When we cry, "Abba! Father!" it is the Spirit himself bearing witness with our spirit that we are children of God, and if children, then heirs, heirs of God and fellow heirs with Christ, provided we suffer with him in order that we may also be glorified with him. (Rom 8:15-17)

The last phrase of Hebrews 1:2 "through whom also he created the world (*tous aiōnas* [the ages])"[6] should not be taken literally, as is done in classical theology influenced by Platonism. Rather, it is imperial terminology.[7] This is corroborated by the fluid expressions "through him" and "in him" that are interchangeable: "for *in him* all things were created, in heaven and on earth, visible and invisible, whether thrones or dominions or principalities or authorities—all things were created *through him* and for him." (Col 1:16) The reference to Christ's "function" at creation is usually done in a context that speaks of his appointment in the place of honor at the end of the scriptural trajectory, wherein he is presented as the fulfiller of the divine plan and thus at the tail end of that plan, so to speak.

The "first-born" (*prōtotokos*) and "heir" (*klēronomos*) are concomitant terms reflective of imperial terminology. In other words, it is upon becoming heir that one is declared first-born and not vice-versa. Until then, the heir is equal to all the slaves in the household, although he is potentially "lord of all": "I mean that the heir, as long as he is a child, *is no better than a slave*, though he is the owner of all the estate (*kyrios pantōn*; lord of all and everything); but he is under guardians and trustees until the date set by the father." (Gal 4:1-2) The imperial context is evident in Hebrews where, after having used "the ages" (*tous*

---

[6] KJV "the worlds."
[7] See my comments on Col 1:15-20 in *C-Col* 43-9.

aiōnas; 1:2) and "all things" (*ta panta*; v.3) to refer to the universe or the world, the author suddenly introduces the technical phrase *tēn oikoumenēn* (the inhabited world, co-extensive with the Roman empire) in v.6 to speak of the same reality: "And again, when he brings the first-born (*ton prōtotokon*) into the world (*tēn oikoumenēn*), he says, 'Let all God's angels worship him.'"

The primacy and thus priority of the "heir" over the "first-born" is evident in Romans where Paul first speaks of Christ as heir and of his addressees as fellow heirs (8:17), and then introduces Christ as "first-born among many brethren" (v.29). Put otherwise, one *is not* preeminent until one accedes to and is "seen" in the position of eminence:

> But in fact Christ has been raised from the dead, the first fruits of those who have fallen asleep. For as by a man came death, by a man has come also the resurrection of the dead. For as in Adam all die, so also in Christ shall all be made alive. But each in his own order: Christ the first fruits, then at his coming those who belong to Christ. Then comes the end, when he delivers the kingdom to God the Father after destroying every rule and every authority and power. For he must reign until he has put all his enemies under his feet. The last enemy to be destroyed is death. "For God has put all things in subjection under his feet." (1 Cor 15:20-27)

> He is the image of the invisible God, the first-born of all creation; for in him all things were created, in heaven and on earth, visible and invisible, whether thrones or dominions or principalities or authorities—all things were created through him and for him. He is before all things, and in him all things hold together. He is the head of the body, the church; he is the beginning, the first-born from the dead, that in everything he might be pre-eminent. (Col 1:15-18)

> Baptism, which corresponds to this, now saves you, not as a removal of dirt from the body but as an appeal to God for a clear conscience, through the resurrection of Jesus Christ, who has gone into heaven and is at the right hand of God, with angels, authorities, and powers subject to him. (1 Pet 3:21-22)

Hence, the preeminence "of the beginning" is a retrojection of the actual one that takes place "at the end." Only linguistically can a monarch or a president be born on such and such a date, for the very simple reason that at birth, one would not have been monarch or president. Even more, being the "first in line" prince is no guarantee that one shall be monarch since one may die before ever becoming king. The same applies to all similar cases, e.g., a president having attended a certain school or, for that matter, having cut down a cherry tree while a teenager. Unfortunately, under the influence of Platonism, whose main anchor is "pre-existence," classical theology started speaking of "eternal" preeminence, a notion that is totally foreign to scripture.[8] "Before birth" is only a metaphor used to emphasize that God's will is without reference to the disposition of any assignee who has no other choice but to submit to that divine will. This is clear from the circumstances of Jeremiah and Paul:

> Now the word of the Lord came to me saying, "Before I formed you in the womb I knew you, and before you were born I consecrated you; I appointed you a prophet to the nations." Then I said, "Ah, Lord God! Behold, I do not know how to speak, for I am only a youth." but the Lord said to me, "Do not say, 'I am only a youth'; for to all to whom I send you you shall go, and whatever I command you you shall speak. Be not afraid of them, for I am with you to deliver you, says the Lord." (Jer 1:4-8)

---

[8] A similar theological oxymoron is noticeable in our speaking of some of us being (somehow) *already* in a "kingdom" that has *not yet* come!

But when he who had set me apart before I was born, and had called me through his grace, was pleased to reveal his Son to me, in order that I might preach him among the Gentiles, I did not confer with flesh and blood, nor did I go up to Jerusalem to those who were apostles before me, but I went away into Arabia; and again I returned to Damascus. (Gal 1:15-17)

It would be sheer [Platonic] madness to assume that Jeremiah was prophet or Paul apostle while they were in their mothers' wombs! That would be tantamount to accepting as a fact of history that George Washington was already the first president of the United States of America before his birth!

One should bear this in mind when hearing and perceiving the following statement concerning the one who *was just appointed as heir in these last days* (Heb 1:2): "Who being the brightness of *his* glory, and the express image of his person, and upholding all things by the word of his power." (KJV v.3a)[9] This description in no way refers to a pre-existent eternal status; rather it is connected to the rest of vv.3b-4: "upholding (*pherōn*) the universe by his word of power. When he had made (*poiēsamenos*; having made) purification for sins, he sat down (*ekathisen*) at the right hand of the Majesty on high, having become (*genomenos*) as much superior to angels as the name he *has obtained* (*keklēronomēken*) is more excellent than theirs." Notice the following:

1. "Upholding" and "having become" are participles paralleling "being" (in the original Greek) at the beginning of v.2, and describing the status the heir acceded to when "he sat down (past tense) at

---

[9] I opted for KJV because it is more literal and thus closer to the original. The italicized "his" is in KJV.

the right hand of the Majesty," which corresponds to "*in these last days* God has spoken (past tense) to us by a Son" (v.2).

2. Since being named "heir" *in these last days* is the reason behind his having become superior to the angels, this status of superiority cannot possibly be an eternal "pre-existent" one.

3. Most importantly, as it will be shown profusely throughout the letter, our purification from sins took place through Christ's sacrificial death, which cannot possibly be an "eternally pre-existent" event or reality. At any rate, that sacrifice took place *after* those sacrifices prescribed in the Law.

The conclusion is unavoidable: all the prerogatives of the "heir," including that of "upholding the universe by his word of power," should be viewed against the background of imperial status. However, this letter is mainly concerned with the priestly function of Jesus Christ, so from the beginning the author includes the sacrificial component (v.3b) of that status. It is important to remember that such a function was not an extraneous component to kingly imperial status. Indeed, Solomon was not only king, but acted as high priest as well. In the Roman empire, as early as the reign of Augustus Caesar, the title of the emperor included *pontifex maximus* (greatest pontiff [priest]). The close link between the two functions of king and priest will be revisited in chapter 5 (vv.5b-6) where, in describing the glorification of Christ by God (v.5a), the author quotes in one breath Psalms 2:7, "Thou art my Son, today I have begotten thee," and 110:4, "Thou art a priest for ever, after the order of Melchizedek."

In classical theology the "angels" (Heb 1:4, 5, 6, 7, 13) came to be viewed as "pre-existent" beings,[10] as were the "thrones or dominions or principalities or authorities" of Colossians 1:16 which were considered levels of the nine "angelic" planes. In actuality, they were metaphoric references to the powers in Jerusalem and in Rome that were acting against the Christ whom Paul was preaching.[11] In other words, the four terms, "thrones or dominions or principalities or authorities," are functional in the immediate context of the text. Similarly, in Hebrews, one must hear the term "angels" against the immediate background of the text. The Greek *angelōn* (Heb 1:4, 5) is the noun complement plural form of *angelos* (angel), which means "messenger," as does its original Hebrew *mal'ak*. This is precisely how RSV translates *angelōn* elsewhere.[12] Hebrews 1:1-4 is intended to compare the "prophets" with the "son" through whom the same God "spoke" or "has spoken" (vv.1-2). The intention is to show the superiority of the son *as messenger* over the prophets *as messengers* and, by the same token, the superiority of the message of "the last days" over the message of earlier times. As we shall see from the letter's content, the superiority does not lie in the difference in content of the messages. The earlier messengers were predicting as well as preparing for the message brought about by the "heir," which is the new covenant (Heb 8:7-13) foretold by the prophet Jeremiah (31:31-34), that is to be shared not only with Israel but also with the entire "habitation" (*oikoumenē*) of the Roman empire. This is corroborated by the ending of chapter

---

[10] Again, this understanding was influenced by Platonism.
[11] See *C-Col* 45-8.
[12] Mt 11:10; Mk 1:2; Lk 7:24, 27; 9:52; 2 Cor 12:7; Jam 2:25.

Chapter 1

1 whereby the mission of the "angels" (v.14) is to prepare for those who are about to obtain "salvation" (*sōterian*) granted by the "savior" (*sōtēr*), "savior" being one of the official imperial titles.

Vv. 5-14 ⁵Τίνι γὰρ εἶπέν ποτε τῶν ἀγγέλων· υἱός μου εἶ σύ, ἐγὼ σήμερον γεγέννηκά σε; καὶ πάλιν· ἐγὼ ἔσομαι αὐτῷ εἰς πατέρα, καὶ αὐτὸς ἔσται μοι εἰς υἱόν; ⁶ ὅταν δὲ πάλιν εἰσαγάγῃ τὸν πρωτότοκον εἰς τὴν οἰκουμένην, λέγει· καὶ προσκυνησάτωσαν αὐτῷ πάντες ἄγγελοι θεοῦ. ⁷καὶ πρὸς μὲν τοὺς ἀγγέλους λέγει· ὁ ποιῶν τοὺς ἀγγέλους αὐτοῦ πνεύματα καὶ τοὺς λειτουργοὺς αὐτοῦ πυρὸς φλόγα, ⁸πρὸς δὲ τὸν υἱόν· ὁ θρόνος σου ὁ θεὸς εἰς τὸν αἰῶνα τοῦ αἰῶνος, καὶ ἡ ῥάβδος τῆς εὐθύτητος ῥάβδος τῆς βασιλείας σου. ⁹ ἠγάπησας δικαιοσύνην καὶ ἐμίσησας ἀνομίαν· διὰ τοῦτο ἔχρισέν σε ὁ θεὸς ὁ θεός σου ἔλαιον ἀγαλλιάσεως παρὰ τοὺς μετόχους σου. ¹⁰καί· σὺ κατ᾽ ἀρχάς, κύριε, τὴν γῆν ἐθεμελίωσας, καὶ ἔργα τῶν χειρῶν σού εἰσιν οἱ οὐρανοί· ¹¹αὐτοὶ ἀπολοῦνται, σὺ δὲ διαμένεις, καὶ πάντες ὡς ἱμάτιον παλαιωθήσονται, ¹²καὶ ὡσεὶ περιβόλαιον ἑλίξεις αὐτούς, ὡς ἱμάτιον καὶ ἀλλαγήσονται· σὺ δὲ ὁ αὐτὸς εἶ καὶ τὰ ἔτη σου οὐκ ἐκλείψουσιν. ¹³πρὸς τίνα δὲ τῶν ἀγγέλων εἴρηκέν ποτε· κάθου ἐκ δεξιῶν μου, ἕως ἂν θῶ τοὺς ἐχθρούς σου ὑποπόδιον τῶν ποδῶν σου; ¹⁴οὐχὶ πάντες εἰσὶν λειτουργικὰ πνεύματα εἰς διακονίαν ἀποστελλόμενα διὰ τοὺς μέλλοντας κληρονομεῖν σωτηρίαν.

⁵*For to what angel did God ever say, "Thou art my Son, today I have begotten thee"? Or again, "I will be to him a father, and he shall be to me a son"?* ⁶*And again, when he brings the first-born into the world, he says, "Let all God's angels worship him."* ⁷*Of the angels he says, "Who makes his angels winds, and his servants flames of fire."* ⁸*But of the Son he says, "Thy throne, O God, is for ever and ever, the righteous scepter is the scepter of thy kingdom.* ⁹*Thou hast loved righteousness and hated lawlessness; therefore God, thy God, has anointed thee with the oil of gladness beyond thy comrades."* ¹⁰*And, "Thou, Lord, didst found the earth in the beginning, and the heavens are the work*

of thy hands; ¹¹they will perish, but thou remainest; they will all grow old like a garment, ¹²like a mantle thou wilt roll them up, and they will be changed. But thou art the same, and thy years will never end." ¹³But to what angel has he ever said, "Sit at my right hand, till I make thy enemies a stool for thy feet"? ¹⁴Are they not all ministering spirits sent forth to serve, for the sake of those who are to obtain salvation?

In v. 5 the "heir" is presented as both the "son of God," Israel's anointed, and the "firstborn" of the "(entire) world" (*tēn oikoumenēn*; v.6), that is of the Roman empire, and in both cases he is compared to the "angels" (vv.6, 7, 13). Although reference is made only to the prophets (v.1), the entirety of scripture is intended. This is confirmed by a similar reference to the prophets in the opening verses of Paul's letter to the Romans:

> Paul, a servant of Jesus Christ, called to be an apostle, set apart for the gospel of God which he promised beforehand through his prophets in the holy scriptures, the gospel concerning his Son, who was descended from David according to the flesh and designated Son of God in power according to the Spirit of holiness by his resurrection from the dead, Jesus Christ our Lord. (1:1-4)

Since the main argument of Hebrews is drawn from scripture (1:1), this epistle is as replete with scriptural quotations, comparable to the letter to the Romans. From the start the author overwhelms his hearers with extensive references (Heb 1:5-2:9) taken almost exclusively from the Book of Psalms, which is the Psalmody of the heavenly Zion temple.[13] The main thesis of Hebrews is that Christ, the new David, *as king* is that temple's high priest. Having established that Christ is the "heir"

---

[13] See *OTI₃* 99-104 and *C-Is* 53-8. See also Paul Tarazi, "David and the Psalter"; *The Journal of the Orthodox Center for the Advancement of Biblical Studies (JOCABS)* Vol.3, No.1 (2010).

on the basis of his appointment as king (Heb 1:5-2:9), the author is able to ease into speaking of him as high priest (2:17).

Whereas the rest of the New Testament revolves around the thesis that Jesus is the Christ, the Anointed one, that is to say, it presents him as the expected "son of David," "son of God," Hebrews is the only book within this literature where the high priesthood of Christ has the lion's share. In order to understand the author's peculiar choice, a digression is in order to elucidate the function of kingship in the Ancient Mediterranean world. When one considers that most of the ancient Near Eastern cities were much smaller than the fortresses of the European Middle Ages and were without streets, one will realize that the area of the city gate, the market place, was the *only* place where citizens and visitors could congregate and exchange ideas as well as trade. Literally, the entire life of the city took place there.[14] The two main buildings that stood at the entrance of the city were the twin "temple" and "palace." Their twin status is reflected in Hebrew that uses the same noun *hekal* for both. The literal meaning of *hekal* is "structure" of either stone or brick. This corresponds to the twin status of deity and monarch; both were known as *melek* (king) whose literal meaning is "owner," "proprietor," and *'ab* (father). As such the *melek* was bound to take care of the citizens, his "children," especially the needy among them (Ps 72:1-4, 12-14; 82:3-4). However, deity and king were not on equal footing regarding the attribute of fatherhood and kingship since the deity was also the "father" and "lord" of the king while the king was merely the deity's "son" and "servant." Graphically put, the monarch was seated on the throne in his palace and, in that

---

[14] Later such activity will take place in the *agora* of the Greek and Hellenistic cities, in the *forum* of Roman cities, in the "square" of the medieval towns, in the "green" of towns and villages, in the *centrum* of modern European cities, and in the downtown "Main Street" of American cities.

position, he was both father and lord of the citizens, his "subjects." But in the temple, although the monarch would be at the head of the people, nonetheless, he would be standing, not sitting, before the deity who would be seated on the throne. Thus even the monarch would be the deity's "subject." This feature of "inequality" is so essential that it applies even to the risen Lord Jesus:

> But in fact Christ has been raised from the dead, the first fruits of those who have fallen asleep. For as by a man came death, by a man has come also the resurrection of the dead. For as in Adam all die, so also in Christ shall all be made alive. But each in his own order: Christ the first fruits, then at his coming those who belong to Christ. Then comes the end, when he delivers the kingdom to God the Father after destroying every rule and every authority and power. For he must reign until he has put all his enemies under his feet. The last enemy to be destroyed is death. "For God has put all things in subjection under his feet." But when it says, "All things are put in subjection under him," it is plain that he is excepted who put all things under him. When all things are subjected to him, then the Son himself will also be subjected to him who put all things under him, that God may be everything to every one. (1 Cor 15:20-28)

At best, the monarch would be seated at God's right hand (Ps 110:1), that is, the second place of honor, as was Jesus upon his exaltation (Mk 16:19; Acts 2:32-33a; 5:31; 7:55-56; Rom 8:34; Eph 1:20; Col 3:1; Heb 1:3).

Still, when the monarch is standing at the head of the people before the seat of the deity in the temple, he has a special function that sets him apart from the rest of the deity's subjects. He is the "high priest" who speaks in as well as on behalf of the people, as Solomon did in his first prayer at the building of the temple (1 Kg 8:22-61). It is precisely this dual functionality of kingship that allows the author of Hebrews to assert that Christ holds the superiority over all preceding divine messengers (Heb ch.1), on the one hand, and that the same Christ, on the other hand, is able to call "brethren" (2:11, 12, 17), and thus make "equal" to him, the members of the congregation at whose head he stands as high priest. Moreover, in concentrating on the primary *hekal* (temple of God) rather than the secondary *hekal* (the kingly palace), the author is able to bring into the picture another aspect of temple worship besides prayer: the atoning sacrifices. This allows him to speak of "salvation" (1:14; 2:3) having been wrought through Christ's sacrificial suffering (v.14) after the manner of Isaiah who introduced God's "servant" (Is 53:11a) as a lamb slaughtered (v.7) to make others righteous (v.11b).

Hebrews can well be considered as an expansion on the theme of Philippians 2:5-11 where Jesus Christ behaved as the "servant" (Greek *doulos*; Hebrew *'ebed*; slave) of God by offering himself as a sacrificial lamb and was granted the kingly title of "Lord" (Greek *kyrios*; Hebrew *'adonay*), which was reserved for God alone (Ps 45:6a).[15] The closeness between Hebrews and Philippians is evident in the extensive use of temple service terminology (Phil 2:17).[16] Moreover, it is the only epistle where Paul introduces himself outright as "servant" (*doulos*; slave, 1:1) instead of "apostle" in view of his later depiction of the "Lord Jesus Christ" as a "servant" (*doulos*; slave, 2:7). Philippians along

---

[15] The original for RSV's "Your divine throne endures for ever and ever" is more accurately reflected in KJV's "Thy throne, O God, *is* for ever and ever." The other Old Testament text that speaks of God's anointed one as "God" is Isaiah 9:6: "For to us a child is born, to us a son is given; and the government will be upon his shoulder, and his name will be called 'Wonderful Counselor, Mighty God, Everlasting Father, Prince of Peace.'"

[16] See my comments on these passages in *C-Phil.*

with Colossians were written to instill in the minds of Gentiles that Jesus Christ, the Lamb of God, is emperor in heaven and on earth. Hebrews, on the other hand, functions as an invitation to the Jews of the diaspora, the "Hebrews," to join their Gentile colleagues in relegating to oblivion the earthly Jerusalem[17] and become children of the Jerusalem above (Gal 4:25-26), whither they are to travel as the place of their "rest" (Heb 4:1, 3), just as their fathers traveled across the wilderness toward a place of "rest" (3:11, 18).

With this in mind, let us examine how the author uses his main source, Psalms, the book of psalmody of the Jerusalem above, to validate his argument. The intentionality of his choice is evident in the first and last quotations (Heb 1:5a and 13). Both are taken from the two enthronization psalms, 2 and 110, the first being strictly kingly, while the second is both kingly and priestly, thus foreshadowing the argument of the letter.[18] Moreover, these two quotations are taken from the first section (Book I [Ps 1-41]) and last section (Book V [Ps 107-150]) of the Book of Psalms, whereas the intervening quotations (Heb 1:6, 7, 8-9, 10-12) come from Books II (Ps 42-72) and IV (Ps 90-106). The impression given the hearers is that the author is covering the entirety of Psalms; put otherwise, the entire Book of Psalms backs up his argument.

The author begins with a rhetorical question, "What angel (which of the angels) did God address as his son?" (Heb 1:5), backed up with two quotations, "Thou art my Son, today I have begotten thee" (Ps 2:7), and "I will be to him a father, and he shall be to me a son" (2 Sam 7:14). The combination of these

---

[17] Jerusalem fell to the Romans in 70 A.D.
[18] See below my comments on Heb 5:5-6.

two quotations is ingenious. Zion and Jerusalem refer to two different realities, the former to God's heavenly city and the latter to his earthly city which was destined to be destroyed. The Book of Psalms begins and ends with reference to Zion (Ps 2:6 and 149:2) rather than to Jerusalem.[19] In Psalm 2, Zion is the holy hill of the one seated in the heavens (2:4), and in Psalm 149 he is its only King: "Let Israel be glad in his Maker, let the sons of Zion rejoice in their King!" (149:2) In Psalm 2:6 the intended king is the new David who is after God's heart. In order to protect David from being the architect of the Jerusalem temple that was doomed to destruction, God's "son" Solomon is the actual builder of that temple (2 Samuel 7:14). Thus, in combining both references, the author is preparing for the warning he is about to issue at the beginning of Hebrews 2 which is the conclusion (Therefore [*Dia touto*]) to what he wrote in chapter 1:

> Therefore we must pay the closer attention to what we have heard, lest we drift away from it. For if the message declared by angels was valid and every transgression or disobedience received a just retribution, how shall we escape if we neglect such a great salvation? It was declared at first by the Lord, and it was attested to us by those who heard him, while God also bore witness by signs and wonders and various miracles and by gifts of the Holy Spirit distributed according to his own will. (2:1-4)

As for the "angels," he cites first a passage from Psalm 96:7 LXX[20] that is said of God and applies to the "son." The Greek reads "Worship him, all ye his angels."[21] Since the king is God's appointee, the author writes, "Let all God's angels worship him"

---

[19] *C-Is* 53, 58.
[20] Which is Ps 97:7 TM (Hebrew).
[21] Often the LXX, in deference to scriptural monotheism, renders the original "gods" into "angels."

(Heb 1:6), the "him" being the first-born of v.5a. However, notice how he also changes the original "his [God's] angels" into "God's angels" to insure that the hearers would not deduce that the angels are the king's and not God's. In order to underscore this reality, a quotation from another psalm is used to confirm that the "angels" are not the king's, but God's obedient servants: "Who makes his angels winds, and his servants flames of fire." (v.7; Ps 104:4). Then, in order to preempt the slightest misunderstanding, in speaking of the "son" he quotes the classic passage from Psalms that addresses the king as "god," then immediately refers to the king's God who anoints him:

> But of the Son he says, "Thy throne, O God, is for ever and ever, the righteous scepter is the scepter of thy kingdom. Thou hast loved righteousness and hated lawlessness; therefore God, *thy God*, has anointed thee with the oil of gladness beyond thy comrades." (Heb 1:8-9; Ps 45:6-7)

By now the hearers are ready to accept another passage from Psalms that is re-routed from God to "heir" (Heb 1:10-12; Ps 102:25-27) without any danger of misunderstanding. Lastly, and to top it all, the author quotes Psalm 110:1 (Heb 1:13) where the earthly "lord" is seated at the highest possible place of honor, at the right hand of the heavenly Lord.

Verse 14 wraps up the introductory first chapter and prepares for the body of the letter. It harks back to the quotation from Psalms in v.7, and iterates that the function of the earlier messengers was to prepare the way for the gift of full inheritance granted through the "heir":

> Who makes his angels (*angelous*; messengers) winds (*pnevmata* [spirits]), and his servants (*leitourgous*; ministers performing a cultic duty) flames of fire. (v.7)

Are they[22] not all ministering (*leitourgika*) spirits (*pnevmata*) sent forth (*apostellomena*; from the verb *apostellein* whence *apostolos* [apostle]) to serve (*diakonian*; table fellowship), for the sake of those who are to obtain (*klēronomein*; inherit) salvation? (v.14)

The phraseology of being sent forth as apostles unto the ministry of table fellowship is the classic terminology Paul uses to speak of his apostolic mission, especially in conjunction with inheritance.[23] Just as "rulers" (*arkhontōn*) in 1 Corinthians (2:6, 8) and "thrones or dominions or principalities (*arkhai*) or authorities" in Colossians (1:16) are aimed at Paul's opponents among the Jewish leadership as well as at the Roman authorities,[24] one can safely surmise that the noun "angels" used here (Heb 1:7, 13-14) is also aimed at those same leaders who were preaching "another Jesus than the one we [Paul] preached" (2 Cor 11:4). This is borne out by the following:

1. Paul refers to himself as "angel" when speaking of his apostolic mission in Galatia: "you know it was because of a bodily ailment that I preached the gospel to you at first; and though my condition was a trial to you, you did not scorn or despise me, but received me as an angel (*angelon*) of God, as Christ Jesus" (Gal 4:13-14).

2. The "other" apostles (2 Cor 11:5) who are peaching "another Jesus" are further described in the following terms: "For such men are false apostles, deceitful workmen, disguising themselves as apostles of Christ. And no wonder,

---

[22] The angels of v.13. The original for "to what angel" (RSV v.13a) is "to which of the angels" (KJV).
[23] See my comments in *C-2Cor* 80-6.
[24] See my comments in *C-1Cor* 55-6 and *C-Col* 43-6.

for even Satan disguises himself as an angel (*angelon*) of light. So it is not strange if his servants also disguise themselves as servants of righteousness." (vv.13-15)

Chapter 2

Vv. 1-4 *¹Διὰ τοῦτο δεῖ περισσοτέρως προσέχειν ἡμᾶς τοῖς ἀκουσθεῖσιν, μήποτε παραρυῶμεν. ²εἰ γὰρ ὁ δι' ἀγγέλων λαληθεὶς λόγος ἐγένετο βέβαιος καὶ πᾶσα παράβασις καὶ παρακοὴ ἔλαβεν ἔνδικον μισθαποδοσίαν, ³πῶς ἡμεῖς ἐκφευξόμεθα τηλικαύτης ἀμελήσαντες σωτηρίας, ἥτις ἀρχὴν λαβοῦσα λαλεῖσθαι διὰ τοῦ κυρίου ὑπὸ τῶν ἀκουσάντων εἰς ἡμᾶς ἐβεβαιώθη, ⁴συνεπιμαρτυροῦντος τοῦ θεοῦ σημείοις τε καὶ τέρασιν καὶ ποικίλαις δυνάμεσιν καὶ πνεύματος ἁγίου μερισμοῖς κατὰ τὴν αὐτοῦ θέλησιν;*

¹Therefore we must pay the closer attention to what we have heard, lest we drift away from it. ²For if the message declared by angels was valid and every transgression or disobedience received a just retribution, ³how shall we escape if we neglect such a great salvation? It was declared at first by the Lord, and it was attested to us by those who heard him, ⁴while God also bore witness by signs and wonders and various miracles and by gifts of the Holy Spirit distributed according to his own will.

Following the lead of all the Pauline letters, the author wants to make sure that the hearers not mistake the superiority of the messenger over that of the message. The reason is very simple: the message of salvation is the same; only the audience has expanded to include the nations as well as Israel. This is reflected in the term *oikoumenē* (world), which was introduced in Hebrews 1:6 and will be used in 2:5. The content of the "word" (*logos*; message) declared (*lalētheis* from the verb *lalein*) through[1]

---

[1] Which is the meaning of the Greek preposition *dia*; both KJV and RSV have "by," which may give the impression that the "message" originated in them. The connotation of the original reflects rather a situation which is aptly rendered in Jeremiah: "The words of Jeremiah ... to whom the word of the Lord came ... Then the Lord put forth his hand and touched my mouth; and the Lord said to me, Behold, I have put my words in your mouth.'" (1:1-2, 9)

the "angels" is no less "valid" (*bebaios*; sure, attested) than the (message of) salvation that was declared (*laleisthai* from the verb *lalein*) through[2] the Lord (Jesus), and "was attested (*ebebaiōthē*) to us by those who heard him, while God also bore witness (*synepimartyrountos*) by signs and wonders and various miracles and by gifts of the Holy Spirit distributed (*merismois*) according to his own will" (Heb 2:3-4).[3] "Therefore we must pay *the closer attention* to what we have heard, lest we drift away from it" (v.1), simply because "we" are living in the period of "these last days" (1:2), the precursor of impending last judgment when "every transgression or disobedience would receive a just retribution" (2:2). One cannot possibly miss the echo of what Paul wrote in Romans:

> Beloved, never avenge (*ekdikountes*) yourselves, but leave it to the wrath of God; for it is written, "Vengeance (*ekdikēsis*) is mine, I will repay (*antapodōsō*), says the Lord" ... Besides this you know what hour it is, how it is full time now for you to wake from sleep. For *salvation* is nearer to us now than when we first believed; the night is far gone, the day is at hand. Let us then cast off the works of darkness and put on the armor of light; let us conduct ourselves becomingly as in the day, not in reveling and drunkenness, not in debauchery and licentiousness, not in quarreling and jealousy. But put on the Lord Jesus Christ, and make no provision for the flesh, to gratify its desires. (12:19; 13:11-14)

Vv. 5-18 ⁵Οὐ γὰρ ἀγγέλοις ὑπέταξεν τὴν οἰκουμένην τὴν μέλλουσαν, περὶ ἧς λαλοῦμεν. ⁶διεμαρτύρατο δέ πού τις λέγων· τί ἐστιν ἄνθρωπος ὅτι μιμνῄσκῃ αὐτοῦ, ἢ υἱὸς ἀνθρώπου ὅτι ἐπισκέπτῃ αὐτόν; ⁷ἠλάττωσας αὐτὸν βραχύ τι παρ' ἀγγέλους, δόξῃ καὶ τιμῇ ἐστεφάνωσας αὐτόν, ⁸πάντα ὑπέταξας ὑποκάτω

---

[2] See previous footnote.
[3] This description resonates with the terminology used repeatedly in Acts and in the Pauline letters.

τῶν ποδῶν αὐτοῦ. ἐν τῷ γὰρ ὑποτάξαι [αὐτῷ] τὰ πάντα οὐδὲν ἀφῆκεν αὐτῷ ἀνυπότακτον. Νῦν δὲ οὔπω ὁρῶμεν αὐτῷ τὰ πάντα ὑποτεταγμένα· ⁹τὸν δὲ βραχύ τι παρ' ἀγγέλους ἠλαττωμένον βλέπομεν Ἰησοῦν διὰ τὸ πάθημα τοῦ θανάτου δόξῃ καὶ τιμῇ ἐστεφανωμένον, ὅπως χάριτι θεοῦ ὑπὲρ παντὸς γεύσηται θανάτου. ¹⁰ἔπρεπεν γὰρ αὐτῷ, δι' ὃν τὰ πάντα καὶ δι' οὗ τὰ πάντα, πολλοὺς υἱοὺς εἰς δόξαν ἀγαγόντα τὸν ἀρχηγὸν τῆς σωτηρίας αὐτῶν διὰ παθημάτων τελειῶσαι.¹¹ὅ τε γὰρ ἁγιάζων καὶ οἱ ἁγιαζόμενοι ἐξ ἑνὸς πάντες· δι' ἣν αἰτίαν οὐκ ἐπαισχύνεται ἀδελφοὺς αὐτοὺς καλεῖν ¹²λέγων· ἀπαγγελῶ τὸ ὄνομά σου τοῖς ἀδελφοῖς μου, ἐν μέσῳ ἐκκλησίας ὑμνήσω σε, ¹³καὶ πάλιν· ἐγὼ ἔσομαι πεποιθὼς ἐπ' αὐτῷ, καὶ πάλιν· ἰδοὺ ἐγὼ καὶ τὰ παιδία ἅ μοι ἔδωκεν ὁ θεός. ¹⁴ Ἐπεὶ οὖν τὰ παιδία κεκοινώνηκεν αἵματος καὶ σαρκός, καὶ αὐτὸς παραπλησίως μετέσχεν τῶν αὐτῶν, ἵνα διὰ τοῦ θανάτου καταργήσῃ τὸν τὸ κράτος ἔχοντα τοῦ θανάτου, τοῦτ' ἔστιν τὸν διάβολον, ¹⁵καὶ ἀπαλλάξῃ τούτους, ὅσοι φόβῳ θανάτου διὰ παντὸς τοῦ ζῆν ἔνοχοι ἦσαν δουλείας. ¹⁶οὐ γὰρ δήπου ἀγγέλων ἐπιλαμβάνεται ἀλλὰ σπέρματος Ἀβραὰμ ἐπιλαμβάνεται. ¹⁷ὅθεν ὤφειλεν κατὰ πάντα τοῖς ἀδελφοῖς ὁμοιωθῆναι, ἵνα ἐλεήμων γένηται καὶ πιστὸς ἀρχιερεὺς τὰ πρὸς τὸν θεὸν εἰς τὸ ἱλάσκεσθαι τὰς ἁμαρτίας τοῦ λαοῦ. ¹⁸ἐν ᾧ γὰρ πέπονθεν αὐτὸς πειρασθείς, δύναται τοῖς πειραζομένοις βοηθῆσαι.

⁵For it was not to angels that God subjected the world to come, of which we are speaking. ⁶It has been testified somewhere, "What is man that thou art mindful of him, or the son of man, that thou carest for him? ⁷Thou didst make him for a little while lower than the angels, thou hast crowned him with glory and honor, ⁸putting everything in subjection under his feet." Now in putting everything in subjection to him, he left nothing outside his control. As it is, we do not yet see everything in subjection to him. ⁹But we see Jesus, who for a little while was made lower than the angels, crowned with glory and honor because of the suffering of death, so that by the grace of God he might taste death for every one. ¹⁰For it was fitting that he, for whom and by whom all things exist, in bringing many sons to glory, should

> make the pioneer of their salvation perfect through suffering. ¹¹For he who sanctifies and those who are sanctified have all one origin. That is why he is not ashamed to call them brethren, ¹²saying, "I will proclaim thy name to my brethren, in the midst of the congregation I will praise thee." ¹³And again, "I will put my trust in him." And again, "Here am I, and the children God has given me." ¹⁴Since therefore the children share in flesh and blood, he himself likewise partook of the same nature, that through death he might destroy him who has the power of death, that is, the devil, ¹⁵and deliver all those who through fear of death were subject to lifelong bondage. ¹⁶For surely it is not with angels that he is concerned but with the descendants of Abraham. ¹⁷Therefore he had to be made like his brethren in every respect, so that he might become a merciful and faithful high priest in the service of God, to make expiation for the sins of the people. ¹⁸For because he himself has suffered and been tempted, he is able to help those who are tempted.

In order to differentiate between the *oikoumenēn* that is under the aegis of the Roman emperor and the expanded realm covered by the "heir," the author labels the world "of which we are speaking" as that "(about) to come" (*tēn mellousan;* v.5), "testified" (*diemartyrato*; attested; v.6) in scripture, that is to say, by the same God who "attested" (*synepimartyrountos*) to "the salvation declared by the Lord" (v.3). He then develops in more detail the point he alluded to in chapter 1: the king or emperor is also the high priest. This approach is along the same line of thought found in Philippians:

> Have this mind among yourselves, which is yours in Christ, who, though he was in the form of God, did not count equality with God a thing to be grasped, but emptied himself, taking the form of a servant, being born in the likeness of men. And being found in human form he humbled himself and became obedient unto

death, even death on a cross. Therefore God has highly exalted him and bestowed on him the name which is above every name, that at the name of Jesus every knee should bow, in heaven and on earth and under the earth, and every tongue confess that Jesus Christ is Lord, to the glory of God the Father. (2:2-11)

What is emphasized in Hebrews, however, is the equality between Christ and his fellow human beings, that is, those he saves, in spite of his superiority over the angels. The phrases "in the form of God" and "equality with God" (Phil 2:6) had in mind the human being Adam as described in Genesis 1[4]:

> Then God said, "Let us make man (*'adam;* Greek *anthrōpon*) in our image, after our likeness; and let them have dominion over the fish of the sea, and over the birds of the air, and over the cattle, and over all the earth, and over every creeping thing that creeps upon the earth." So God created man (*ha'adam*; Greek *ton anthrōpon*; the human being) in his own image, in the image of God he created *him*;[5] male and female he created *them*. (vv.26-27)

A digression on the word play between the Hebrew and Greek is in order here. The Hebrew *'adam* is a noun meaning "human being" in general and thus connotes every human being, male or female, as is evident from v.27. That is why *'adam* is often preceded by the definite article *ha[l]* as is the case in that verse. Greek differentiates between "man" and "the man" by using *anthrōpon* in the first case and *ton anthrōpon* in the second. This explains why the first human being's proper name is *'adam* (Adam)[6] and, consequently, his progeny is *ben 'adam* (son of Adam; child [descendant] of Adam) and their totality *bene 'adam* (sons of Adam; children [descendants] of Adam). Another

---

[4] See *C- Phil* 128-133.
[5] The Hebrew noun *'adam* is grammatically masculine.
[6] The Hebrew has no upper case letters.

corollary is that, whenever *'adam* appears without the definite article, translations, including the LXX, have no choice but to tergiversate between Adam and "man," losing the "edge" of the word play in Hebrew. By the same token, translations cannot possibly differentiate between *bene 'adam* (children of man/Adam) and *bene ha'adam* (children of *the* human being).

Keeping this in mind, one can understand the author's ingenuity in quoting from Psalm 8 to start the point aimed at in Hebrews 2:

> What is man (Hebrew *'enoš*;[7] Greek *anthrōpos*) that thou art mindful of him, and the son of man (Hebrew *ben 'adam*; Greek *hyios anthrōpou*) that thou dost care for him? Yet thou hast made him *little less* (*brakhy ti*) than God (*'elohim*; gods), and dost crown him with glory and honor. Thou hast given him dominion over the works of thy hands; thou hast put all things under his feet. (Ps 8:4-6)

> What is man (*anthrōpos*) that thou art mindful of him, or the son of man (*hyios anthrōpou*), that thou carest for him? Thou didst make him *for a little while lower* (*brakhy ti*) than the angels,[8] thou hast crowned him with glory and honor, putting everything in subjection under his feet." (Heb 2:6b-8a)

---

[7] Another noun meaning "human being" (e.g. Job 5:17; 7:17; Ps 9:19; 10:18), which is also used as a proper name in Genesis 4:25-26: "And Adam (Hebrew *'adam*; Greek *Adam*) knew his wife again, and she bore a son and called his name Seth, for she said, 'God has appointed for me another child instead of Abel, for Cain slew him.' To Seth also a son was born, and he called his name Enosh (Hebrew *'enoš*; Greek *Enōs*). At that time men began to call upon the name of the Lord." The full correspondence between *'adam* and *'enoš* is evident in how both nouns can be used as proper names of progenitors.

[8] As I mentioned above, usually the LXX prefers to use "angels" for "gods." The Hebrew *'elohim* can mean either "God" or "gods," depending on the context. In this particular case, both possibilities work.

This passage in Hebrews allows the author to cover several bases in his argument. As in Philippians, a mere human being is elevated to the highest possible rank, the divine rank, surpassing even the angels that are "higher than" or "before" him. At any rate, by applying this assertion to Jesus (v.9), which in Hebrew means "the Lord has saved," and presenting him as "the pioneer of the salvation of many sons whom he brings to glory" (v.10), the author can then explain how the salvation of the many (1:14) is realized. The intentional use of "Jesus" here is borne out by the fact that it appears on its own three times (2:9; 3:1, 3) before the first reference to him as "Christ" in 3:6. This is, to say the least, unusual in Paul. Moreover, one would have expected that "Christ" be mentioned sooner than this, especially in conjunction with the many passages from Psalms that refers to God's "anointed" in chapter 1.[9] Using "Jesus" allows the author to speak of the pioneer of the salvation "for every one" (2:9) as a "brother" (v.11) and thus on equal footing with his addressees. It is precisely this relationship that allows the author to move to that other aspect of kingship, that of high priest. The high priest is not in fact higher or superior to the rest of the members of the congregation since he has to atone for his own sins as well as for those of the people, a point that was already introduced in 1:3b and will be expanded on later in the text:

> For every high priest chosen from among men is appointed to act on behalf of men in relation to God, to offer gifts and sacrifices for sins. He can deal gently with the ignorant and wayward, since he himself is beset with weakness. Because of this he is bound to offer sacrifice for his own sins as well as for those of the people. And one does not take the honor upon himself, but he is called by God, just as Aaron was. (5:1-4)

---

[9] The Greek *Khristos* literally means "anointed."

The second set of quotations in 2:12-13 reinforces the statement in v.8b: "As it is, we do not yet see everything in subjection to him." Such requires hope with patience in the midst of sufferings on the way to perfection. This is vintage Paul, especially since the leader himself is not exempt from such sufferings (v.10). The quotations are from the lips of leaders who, together with the community around them, have to await God's promised intervention. Rather than despair, in the midst of their suffering they each proclaim their assurance that, in his time, God's promise shall be fulfilled: "I will proclaim thy name to my brethren, in the midst of the congregation (*ekklēsias*; church) I will praise thee" (v.12); "I will put my trust in him ... Here am I, and the children God has given me." (v.13) The first quotation (v. 12) is from Psalm 22:22, which is the turning point in this lengthy psalm; the first half (vv.1-21) is filled with complaints on the part of someone whom God seemingly left to destruction, while the second half (vv.22-31) resounds of determined hope and culminates with "Posterity shall serve him [the Lord]; men shall tell of the Lord to the coming generation, and proclaim his deliverance to a people yet unborn, that he has wrought it." (vv.30-31). The following quotation (Heb. 2:13) is from Isaiah 8:17a-18b where the prophet looks ahead to the vindication of God's words to him among the upcoming generations, in spite of the recalcitrance of those around him:

> Bind up the testimony, seal the teaching among my disciples. I will wait for the Lord, who is hiding his face from the house of Jacob, and I will hope in him. Behold, I and the children whom the Lord has given me are signs and portents in Israel from the Lord of hosts, who dwells on Mount Zion. (vv.16-18)

By underscoring the "brotherhood" between Jesus and the addressees (Heb 2:10-11), the author is preparing for the climax of the entire passage (vv.5-18), that is, Jesus' function as high priest (v.17). He does this by bringing into the picture the element of sanctification (v.11), which is a priestly prerogative: "For he who sanctifies and those who are sanctified have all one origin (*ex henos pantes*; KJV are all of one)." The peculiar closing phrase, "all one origin," is not simply happenstance, but clearly has in mind "the descendants (*spermatos*; progeny) of Abraham" (v.16b). Later in the letter (chs.6-7) Abraham will be dealt with extensively in conjunction with Melchizedek "the priest" (7:1). Indeed, the brotherhood between Jesus and the addressees is "so that he [Jesus] might become a merciful and faithful high priest in the service of God, to make expiation for the sins of the people." (2:17)

Still, there is more here than meets the ear. The quotation concerning Abraham is taken from Isaiah 41:8-9 and surmises on the quotation from Psalms in Hebrews 2:12 through the reference to "brethren," respectively "children," and the hope of salvation in the future. Referencing Isaiah works on two levels. On the one hand, Isaiah is strikingly divided into two sections: chapters 1-39 and chapters 40-66, which content wise function as promise and fulfillment.[10] So by using a quotation from Isaiah 8:17-18 (Heb 2:13) followed by one from Isaiah 41:8-9 (Heb 2:16), the hearers are invited to perceive that the hope (vv.12-13) was realized and that God does keep his promise. On the other hand, up to this point all the quotations are taken from Psalms, the first book of the Writings (*ketubim*) and thus representative of the third part of the Old Testament scripture. Since Isaiah is the first book of the Latter Prophets, it functions as *pars pro toto* of the second part of the Old Testament scripture, the Prophets (*nebi'im*). Furthermore, specifically opting for a quotation

---

[10] See *C-Is* 89, 192.

concerning "the descendants (*spermatos*; progeny) of Abraham" deftly brings to mind Genesis, which is the first book of the Law (*torah*), the first part of the Old Testament scripture. This prepares for the reference to Moses and the wilderness trek in Hebrews 3-4, and then to Abraham and Melchizedek in chapters 5-7. Thus, the hearer perceives that the entire scripture bears witness to the author's argument, which is the stratagem Paul uses in Romans.[11]

Although the monarch appears in his palace to be lord over his people, when in the temple as the high priest he stands with the people and thus appears as one of them before God. In presenting Jesus as high priest (Heb 2:17), the author capitalizes on the aspect of equality between Jesus and his "brethren." He starts the passage (vv. 14-18) stressing what they have in common, "flesh and blood." By using the term "nature," RSV injected into the text the notion of "incarnation" that pervaded later theology.[12] However, when heard in the original against the background of Roman socio-polity, one realizes that the setting is the Roman arena. This is the case throughout the Pauline epistles, especially in the Corinthian correspondence. In this setting the "divine" emperor has the ultimate authority over the life and death of the *morituri* (deathbound; Greek *thnētoi*)[13] gladiators who are mere "human," devoid of control over their own lives—in scriptural terminology, over their own "flesh and blood."[14] This is confirmed in v.14b where the main antagonist, twice mentioned, is "death," which is put under the aegis of God's nemesis, the devil. In order to prepare for the move into

---

[11] See my comments in *C-Rom* 192, 200, 260-1.
[12] KJV (and so does JB) reads: "Forasmuch then as the children are partakers of flesh and blood, he also himself likewise took part of the same."
[13] See 2 Cor 4:11; 5:4 and my comments in *C-2Cor*.
[14] See e.g. "flesh and blood" in Mt 16:17; Jn 1:13; Gal 1:16; Eph 6:12.

the scriptural world, v.15 compares death in the arena to the "bondage" (in Egypt)[15] that required "salvation" wrought by God. Both bondage and salvation are matters that do not concern "angels" but rather human beings, "the progeny of Abraham" (v.16), whom God brought out of Egypt (v.15).

Whenever the people commit sins that would warrant their exile into bondage, it would be the function of the high priest to make expiation for those sins (v.17c). However, the high priest himself, being one of the brethren (v.17a), is confronted with similar temptations (v.18) and has to expiate for himself as well as for the people (9:7). Therefore, while he is to be "faithful in the service of God" he ought at the same time to be "merciful" toward his brethren (v.17b). And this is how Jesus, as high priest, is depicted. Later in the letter, the author will again address this matter to affirm that the aspect of compassion is all the more present in Jesus when compared to the Old Testament high priests because, though he shared the temptations of his brethren, he committed no sin (4:15).

---

[15] This unique instance of *douleia* (bondage; slavery; servitude) in Hebrews corresponds to its use in Gal 4:24 where we hear of the Jerusalem above (v.26) that will be referred to in Heb 12:22.

Chapter 3

Vv. 1-6 ¹Ὅθεν, ἀδελφοὶ ἅγιοι, κλήσεως ἐπουρανίου μέτοχοι, κατανοήσατε τὸν ἀπόστολον καὶ ἀρχιερέα τῆς ὁμολογίας ἡμῶν Ἰησοῦν, ² πιστὸν ὄντα τῷ ποιήσαντι αὐτὸν ὡς καὶ Μωϋσῆς ἐν [ὅλῳ] τῷ οἴκῳ αὐτοῦ. ³πλείονος γὰρ οὗτος δόξης παρὰ Μωϋσῆν ἠξίωται, καθ᾽ ὅσον πλείονα τιμὴν ἔχει τοῦ οἴκου ὁ κατασκευάσας αὐτόν· ⁴πᾶς γὰρ οἶκος κατασκευάζεται ὑπό τινος, ὁ δὲ πάντα κατασκευάσας θεός. ⁵καὶ Μωϋσῆς μὲν πιστὸς ἐν ὅλῳ τῷ οἴκῳ αὐτοῦ ὡς θεράπων εἰς μαρτύριον τῶν λαληθησομένων, ⁶Χριστὸς δὲ ὡς υἱὸς ἐπὶ τὸν οἶκον αὐτοῦ· οὗ οἶκός ἐσμεν ἡμεῖς, ἐάν[περ] τὴν παρρησίαν καὶ τὸ καύχημα τῆς ἐλπίδος κατάσχωμεν.

¹Therefore, holy brethren, who share in a heavenly call, consider Jesus, the apostle and high priest of our confession. ²He was faithful to him who appointed him, just as Moses also was faithful in God's house. ³Yet Jesus has been counted worthy of as much more glory than Moses as the builder of a house has more honor than the house. ⁴(For every house is built by some one, but the builder of all things is God.) ⁵Now Moses was faithful in all God's house as a servant, to testify to the things that were to be spoken later, ⁶but Christ was faithful over God's house as a son. And we are his house if we hold fast our confidence and pride in our hope.

Now that he introduced the Law through the mention of Abraham (2:16), the author proceeds to compare Jesus with Moses in preparation for his discussion of the new covenant versus the earlier one (ch.8). Hebrews 3:1-5 is an echo of the Pauline teaching, beginning with v.1 that sets the tone. This verse is constructed magisterially: two trademark terms of Hebrews, *metokhoi* (those who share; sharers) in v.1a and "high priest" in v.1b, are surrounded by heavily Pauline vocabulary. *metokhoi* was introduced in 1:9 as part of a quotation from Psalm 45:

Thy throne, O God, is for ever and ever, the righteous scepter is the scepter of thy kingdom. Thou hast loved righteousness and hated lawlessness; therefore God, thy God, has anointed thee with the oil of gladness beyond thy comrades (*metokhous*). (Ps 45:6-7; Heb 1:8-9)

Those "comrades," earlier referred to as "brethren" (2:11, 12, 17), which is a specific Pauline term, allows the author to start chapter 3 with "Therefore, holy (*hagioi*) brethren (*adelphoi*), who share (*metokhoi*; sharers, comrades) in a heavenly (*epouraniou*) call (*klēseōs*)." (v.1a) Except for *metokhoi*, all the other words are thoroughly Pauline. On the other hand, the reference to Jesus as apostle in v.1b is unique in the New Testament, and yet not that unexpected when one considers that in this literature Jesus Christ is cast in the traits of Paul.[1] The highest evidence of this is in 2 Corinthians 3 where the "face of Christ" in Corinth is tantamount to Paul's teaching there.[2] In that chapter the key word is "table ministry" (*diakonia*) which is the term Paul uses to describe his ministry as well as that of Moses.[3] Furthermore, Paul refers to himself as much as *diakonos* (table minister) as *doulos* (servant, slave).[4] In Romans, Paul introduces himself as *the* apostle to the nations, and refers to Christ as "minister to the circumcision" (*diakonon peritomēs*; 15:8). This dual ministry to the Jews and the Gentiles is reflected in Luke's double volume where Jesus ministers in Palestine in the Gospel Book and Paul carries the same message throughout the Roman empire in the Book of Acts.[5] However, what is relevant for our discussion is

---

[1] See my New Testament Introduction tetralogy NTI_1, NTI_2, NTI_3, NTI_4.
[2] See my comments in *C-2Cor* 46-56.
[3] See *C-2Cor* 69-86.
[4] 2 Cor 3:6; 4:5.
[5] See my comments in *C-Rom* 262-3.

that in Romans Paul depicts himself as the high priest of the nations:

> But on some points I have written to you very boldly by way of reminder, because of the grace given me by God to be a minister (*leitourgon*; liturgy, performer of a temple priestly service) of Christ Jesus to the Gentiles in the priestly service of (*hierourgounta* [from the same root as *arkhierea*—high priest in Heb 3:1b]; performing as a priestly service) the gospel of God, so that the offering of the Gentiles may be acceptable, sanctified by the Holy Spirit. In Christ Jesus, then, I have reason to be proud of my work for God. For I will not venture to speak of anything except what Christ has wrought through me to win obedience from the Gentiles, by word and deed, by the power of signs and wonders,[6] by the power of the Holy Spirit, so that from Jerusalem and as far round as Illyricum I have fully preached the gospel of Christ, thus making it my ambition to preach the gospel, not where Christ has already been named, lest I build on another man's foundation. (Rom 15:15-20)

Recalling that Paul wrote early on in Galatians that his center of reference was not the "present Jerusalem" (4:25; see also earlier 1:17), but the "Jerusalem above" (4:26), then one gets the distinct impression that the "heavenly call" (Heb 3:1a) originated in the latter, which is precisely what Paul declared uncompromisingly in Galatians:

> For I would have you know, brethren, that the gospel which was preached by me is not man's gospel. For I did not receive it from man, nor was I taught it, but it came through a revelation of Jesus Christ. For you have heard of my former life in Judaism, how I persecuted the church of God violently and tried to destroy it; and

---

[6] Notice the similarity with Heb 2:4: "while God also bore witness by signs and wonders and various miracles and by gifts of the Holy Spirit distributed according to his own will."

I advanced in Judaism beyond many of my own age among my people, so extremely zealous was I for the traditions of my fathers. But when he who had set me apart before I was born, and had called me through his grace, was pleased to reveal his Son to me, in order that I might preach him among the Gentiles, I did not confer with flesh and blood, nor did I go up to Jerusalem to those who were apostles before me, but I went away into Arabia; and again I returned to Damascus. (1:11-17)

Consequently, the use of "heavenly" (*epouraniou*; Heb 3:1a) looks ahead to the end of the letter. The hearers realize that if the "call" is heavenly," it is because the end of the road trod by those who hearken to that call is none other than "Mount Zion and the city of the living God, the heavenly (*epouraniō*) Jerusalem" (12:22), at whose altar Paul as well as Jesus serves as "high priest."

In my studies on the Gospels, Acts, and Revelation,[7] as well as in my commentaries on the Pauline epistles,[8] I have consistently maintained that the letter to the churches of Galatia functioned as the blue print for the entire New Testament literature. This is clearly evident in Hebrews. The phraseology and structure of 3:1-6 clearly betray the showdown between the apostle Paul and the leaders of Jerusalem and its temple (Gal 1-2). In Hebrews 3:1, though passing and apparently not central to the overall concern of the letter, the function of Jesus as apostle is given priority over that of high priest. This can be detected in the elaboration on that theme in vv.2-6. Since reaching the promised "rest" in the heavenly Jerusalem as well as in Canaan, the earth of the promise, will depend on following the will of God, before introducing the high priest Aaron (5:4; 7:11) and comparing

---

[7] *NTI₁, NTI₂, NTI₃, NTI₄*.
[8] *C-Rom, C-1Cor, C-2Cor, C-Phil, C-Col*.

him with Jesus, the author puts Jesus in parallel with Moses the lawgiver (3:2, 3, 5, 16). The primacy of Moses is evident in that it is he who both institutes the high priesthood through his brother Aaron and issues the rules pertaining to the priestly service in general. Moreover, Moses is privy to the vision of the heavenly sanctuary; Aaron and his colleagues would be ministers of a copy thereof, a matter that will be broached later in the letter (Heb 8-9). The point of parallelism between Moses and Jesus as "messengers" from God is their faithfulness or trustworthiness (Heb 3:2, 5), which is reminiscent of Paul's description of true apostleship: "This is how one should regard us, as servants of Christ and stewards of the mysteries of God. Moreover it is required of stewards that they be found trustworthy (*pistos*)." (1 Cor 4:1-2) The superiority of the apostolic word as the foundation of the liturgical service of the heavenly Zion, over service of the earthly Jerusalem temple, is further evident in the use of the verb *kataskevazein* (translated as "build") that occurs no less than three times to speak of God as "builder" of the *oikos* (house, household; vv.3, 5).

All this imagery harks back to 1 Corinthians 3 where we hear that Paul laid the foundation for the building; the "stones," however, are the actual members of the church community at Corinth who, in turn, are referred to as God's temple:

> According to the grace of God given to me, like a skilled master builder I laid a foundation, and another man is building upon it (*epikodomei*). Let each man take care how he builds upon it (*epikodomei*). For no other foundation can any one lay than that which is laid, which is Jesus Christ ... Do you not know that you are God's temple and that God's Spirit dwells among[9] you? If any

---

[9] RSV has "in."

one destroys God's temple, God will destroy him. For God's temple is holy, and that temple you are. (vv.10-11, 16-17)

The author of Hebrews surmises on this metaphor by exchanging the verb *epikodomein* with *kataskevazein*, a verb that occurs only in Hebrews in the Pauline corpus. Its importance for our discussion is that similar to its counterpart *epikodomein*, a verb formed from the same root as the noun *oikos*, the verb *kataskevazein* is from the same root as the noun *skevos*, which means "vessel" and, more specifically, a temple vessel. Thus *kataskevazein* would have the connotation of "fully refurbish (with vessels)," which is clearly temple terminology. This is corroborated in chapter 9 where the same verb is used twice in conjunction with the tent of meeting: "For a tent was prepared (*kataskevasthē*), the outer one, in which were the lampstand and the table and the bread of the Presence; it is called the Holy Place ... These preparations having thus been made (*kataskevasmenōn*), the priests go continually into the outer tent, performing their ritual duties." (vv.2, 6) So, in using that verb in conjunction with the "house" of Christ (3:6) as well as with the "house" of Moses (v.4), the author is preparing for a final statement that rejoins "you are God's temple" of 1 Corinthians 3:16-17: "Christ was faithful over God's house as a son. And we are his house." (Heb 3:6a) Finally, he ends with another typically Pauline "twist," namely, the assertion of full assuredness is always on hope that constantly looks ahead until the full realization of that assuredness at the coming of God's kingdom: "And we are his house *if* (*eanper*) we hold fast (*kataskhōmen* from the verb *katekhein*) our confidence and pride in our hope." (v.6b) Compare this with the classic teaching of Romans:

> Therefore, since we are justified by faith, we have peace with God through our Lord Jesus Christ. Through him we have obtained

access to this grace in which we stand, and we rejoice in our hope of sharing the glory of God. More than that, we rejoice in our sufferings, knowing that suffering produces endurance, and endurance produces character, and character produces hope, and hope does not disappoint us, because God's love has been poured into our hearts through the Holy Spirit which has been given to us. (5:1-5)

... it is the Spirit himself bearing witness with our spirit that we are children of God, and if children, then heirs, heirs of God and fellow heirs with Christ, provided (*eiper*) we suffer with him in order that we may also be glorified with him ... For in this hope we were saved. Now hope that is seen is not hope. For who hopes for what he sees? But if we hope for what we do not see, we wait for it with patience. (8:16-17, 24-25)

Such thought pervades the letter to the Hebrews itself, and chapter 3 is built up around that teaching. The verb *katekhein* (hold fast; 3:6) that is repeated in v.14 occurs later in the letter in a verse replete with the vocabulary of 3:1-2 and the concluding verse 4:1 to chapter 3:

Let us *hold fast* the *confession* of our *hope* without wavering, for he who *promised* is *faithful*. (10:23)

Therefore, holy brethren, who share in a heavenly call, consider Jesus, the apostle and high priest of our *confession*. He was *faithful* to him who appointed him, just as Moses also was faithful in God's house. (3:1-2)

Therefore, while the *promise* of entering his rest remains, let us fear lest any of you be judged to have failed to reach it. (4:1)[10]

---

[10] Notice how this conclusion alludes to the conditionality of the assuredness of the divine promise.

The same applies to the two instances of the verb *kratein* that also means "hold fast (to), seize" used in chapter 4 and found later in the letter:

> Since then we have a great high priest who has passed through the heavens, Jesus, the Son of God, let us hold fast (*kratōmen*) our *confession*. (4:14)

> So when God desired to show more convincingly to the heirs[11] of the *promise* the unchangeable character of his purpose, he interposed with an oath, so that through two unchangeable things, in which it is impossible that God should prove false, we who have fled for refuge might have strong encouragement to seize (*kratēsai*) the *hope* set before us. (6:17-18)

Vv. 7-19 *⁷Διό, καθὼς λέγει τὸ πνεῦμα τὸ ἅγιον· σήμερον ἐὰν τῆς φωνῆς αὐτοῦ ἀκούσητε, ⁸μὴ σκληρύνητε τὰς καρδίας ὑμῶν ὡς ἐν τῷ παραπικρασμῷ κατὰ τὴν ἡμέραν τοῦ πειρασμοῦ ἐν τῇ ἐρήμῳ, ⁹οὗ ἐπείρασαν οἱ πατέρες ὑμῶν ἐν δοκιμασίᾳ καὶ εἶδον τὰ ἔργα μου ¹⁰τεσσεράκοντα ἔτη· διὸ προσώχθισα τῇ γενεᾷ ταύτῃ καὶ εἶπον· ἀεὶ πλανῶνται τῇ καρδίᾳ, αὐτοὶ δὲ οὐκ ἔγνωσαν τὰς ὁδούς μου, ¹¹ὡς ὤμοσα ἐν τῇ ὀργῇ μου· εἰ εἰσελεύσονται εἰς τὴν κατάπαυσίν μου. ¹²Βλέπετε, ἀδελφοί, μήποτε ἔσται ἔν τινι ὑμῶν καρδία πονηρὰ ἀπιστίας ἐν τῷ ἀποστῆναι ἀπὸ θεοῦ ζῶντος, ¹³ἀλλὰ παρακαλεῖτε ἑαυτοὺς καθ' ἑκάστην ἡμέραν, ἄχρις οὗ τὸ σήμερον καλεῖται, ἵνα μὴ σκληρυνθῇ τις ἐξ ὑμῶν ἀπάτῃ τῆς ἁμαρτίας- ¹⁴μέτοχοι γὰρ τοῦ Χριστοῦ γεγόναμεν, ἐάνπερ τὴν ἀρχὴν τῆς ὑποστάσεως μέχρι τέλους βεβαίαν κατάσχωμεν- ¹⁵ἐν τῷ λέγεσθαι· σήμερον ἐὰν τῆς φωνῆς αὐτοῦ ἀκούσητε, μὴ σκληρύνητε τὰς καρδίας ὑμῶν ὡς ἐν τῷ παραπικρασμῷ. ¹⁶τίνες γὰρ ἀκούσαντες παρεπίκραναν; ἀλλ' οὐ πάντες οἱ ἐξελθόντες ἐξ Αἰγύπτου διὰ Μωϋσέως; ¹⁷τίσιν δὲ προσώχθισεν τεσσεράκοντα ἔτη; οὐχὶ τοῖς ἁμαρτήσασιν, ὧν τὰ κῶλα ἔπεσεν ἐν τῇ ἐρήμῳ; ¹⁸τίσιν δὲ ὤμοσεν μὴ εἰσελεύσεσθαι εἰς τὴν κατάπαυσιν αὐτοῦ εἰ*

---

[11] As "brethren of Christ" (1:2; 2:11, 12, 17).

μὴ τοῖς ἀπειθήσασιν; ¹⁹καὶ βλέπομεν ὅτι οὐκ ἠδυνήθησαν εἰσελθεῖν δι' ἀπιστίαν.

> ⁷Therefore, as the Holy Spirit says, "Today, when you hear his voice, ⁸do not harden your hearts as in the rebellion, on the day of testing in the wilderness, ⁹where your fathers put me to the test and saw my works for forty years. ¹⁰Therefore I was provoked with that generation, and said, 'They always go astray in their hearts; they have not known my ways.' ¹¹As I swore in my wrath, 'They shall never enter my rest.'" ¹²Take care, brethren, lest there be in any of you an evil, unbelieving heart, leading you to fall away from the living God. ¹³But exhort one another every day, as long as it is called "today," that none of you may be hardened by the deceitfulness of sin. ¹⁴For we share in Christ, if only we hold our first confidence firm to the end, ¹⁵while it is said, "Today, when you hear his voice, do not harden your hearts as in the rebellion." ¹⁶Who were they that heard and yet were rebellious? Was it not all those who left Egypt under the leadership of Moses? ¹⁷And with whom was he provoked forty years? Was it not with those who sinned, whose bodies fell in the wilderness? ¹⁸And to whom did he swear that they should never enter his rest, but to those who were disobedient? ¹⁹So we see that they were unable to enter because of unbelief.

The introduction of the element "hope" at the end of 3:6 reminds the hearers that their sharing in the heavenly call (v.1) has not yet been realized and thus is conditional. The importance of this thought is examined in the second part of the chapter (vv.7-19) that discusses the matter in detail. Following his lead from the beginning of the letter, the author quotes lengthily from the Book of Psalms (vv.7a-11; Ps 95:7a-11). However, instead of referring to the anointed heir and the hoped for future under his aegis, the chosen quotation refers to the times of Moses in the wilderness, when the people did *not* hearken to God's voice and, consequently, did *not* attain the promised rest in Canaan, but rather incurred God's wrath and perished in the wilderness. Evidently, what applied to the "house" of Moses, one of God's servants, applies all the more to the "house" of the heir, Christ. The "today" of scripture remains in effect throughout the generations of hearers who are always hearing the text in their own "today." Actually, the author himself points that out: "But exhort one another every day, as long as it is called "today," that none of you may be hardened by the deceitfulness of sin." (Heb 3:13) That the thought was on the author's mind all along can be seen in the introductory formula to the quotation from Psalm 95: "Therefore, as the Holy Spirit says." (Heb 3:7a) On the one hand, the originator of the psalmist's word is none other than the Holy Spirit who was earlier introduced as the agent of the divine interventions that witnessed as well as attested to the apostolic preaching, which in turn puts an even higher level of pressure on the recipients of that message:

> Therefore we must pay the closer attention to what we have heard, lest we drift away from it. For if the message declared by angels was valid and every transgression or disobedience received a just retribution, how shall we escape if we neglect such a great salvation? It was declared at first by the Lord, and it was attested to us by those who heard him, while God also bore witness by signs and wonders and various miracles and by gifts of the Holy Spirit distributed according to his own will. (2:1-4)

On the other hand, the same level of pressure is maintained on the hearers in that the action of the Spirit speaking the psalmist's words is rendered in the present tense *legei* (says, is saying) rather than in the past tense *eipen* (said). So the addressees of the psalmist's words are none other than the hearers of the letter, which is confirmed by the last statement of the chapter: "So *we see* that *they* were unable to enter because of unbelief." (3:19) This approach is reminiscent of Galatians where, after having referred to the Spirit as the guarantor of the assuredness of justification and salvation through faith (2:16-17; 3:1-5, 24), Paul nevertheless relegates the bestowing of that righteousness to the future: "For through the Spirit, by faith, we *wait* for the *hope* of righteousness." (5:5) Similarly, the "fruit" that the Spirit is working in the Galatians (5:22-23) does not release them from the Pauline caveat: "I warn you, as I warned you before, that those who do such things[12] shall not inherit the kingdom of God." (v.21) Paul's influence is also manifest in terminology reminiscent of 1 Thessalonians:

> But exhort (*parakaleite*) one another every day, as long as it is called "today," that none of you may be hardened by the deceitfulness of sin. (Heb 3:13)
>
> Therefore comfort (*parakaleite*) one another with these words. (1 Thess 4:18)
>
> Therefore encourage (*parakaleite*) one another and build one another up, just as you are doing. (1 Thess 5:11)

The connection is beyond doubt since these are the only three instances of *parakaleite* (imperative plural of the verb *parakalein*) in the entire New Testament. A further indication that 1 Thessalonians was on the author's mind here is the reference to the "living God" from whom one "falls away" (Heb 3:12) after having left the idols to turn to him: "For they themselves report concerning us what a welcome we had among you, and how you turned to God from idols, to serve a living and true God." (1 Thess 1:9). Later in Hebrews one hears about "serving" the

---

[12] The works of the flesh, whose "desires are against the Spirit" (v.17a).

living God: "... how much more shall the blood of Christ, who through the eternal Spirit offered himself without blemish to God, purify your conscience from dead works to serve the living God." (9:14)

Chapter 4

Vv. 1-13 *¹φοβηθῶμεν οὖν, μήποτε καταλειπομένης ἐπαγγελίας εἰσελθεῖν εἰς τὴν κατάπαυσιν αὐτοῦ δοκῇ τις ἐξ ὑμῶν ὑστερηκέναι. ²καὶ γάρ ἐσμεν εὐηγγελισμένοι καθάπερ κἀκεῖνοι· ἀλλ᾽ οὐκ ὠφέλησεν ὁ λόγος τῆς ἀκοῆς ἐκείνους μὴ συγκεκερασμένους τῇ πίστει τοῖς ἀκούσασιν. ³Εἰσερχόμεθα γὰρ εἰς [τὴν] κατάπαυσιν οἱ πιστεύσαντες, καθὼς εἴρηκεν· ὡς ὤμοσα ἐν τῇ ὀργῇ μου· εἰ εἰσελεύσονται εἰς τὴν κατάπαυσίν μου, καίτοι τῶν ἔργων ἀπὸ καταβολῆς κόσμου γενηθέντων. ⁴εἴρηκεν γάρ που περὶ τῆς ἑβδόμης οὕτως· καὶ κατέπαυσεν ὁ θεὸς ἐν τῇ ἡμέρᾳ τῇ ἑβδόμῃ ἀπὸ πάντων τῶν ἔργων αὐτοῦ, ⁵καὶ ἐν τούτῳ πάλιν· εἰ εἰσελεύσονται εἰς τὴν κατάπαυσίν μου. ⁶ἐπεὶ οὖν ἀπολείπεται τινὰς εἰσελθεῖν εἰς αὐτήν, καὶ οἱ πρότερον εὐαγγελισθέντες οὐκ εἰσῆλθον δι᾽ ἀπείθειαν, ⁷πάλιν τινὰ ὁρίζει ἡμέραν, σήμερον, ἐν Δαυὶδ λέγων μετὰ τοσοῦτον χρόνον, καθὼς προείρηται· σήμερον ἐὰν τῆς φωνῆς αὐτοῦ ἀκούσητε, μὴ σκληρύνητε τὰς καρδίας ὑμῶν. ⁸εἰ γὰρ αὐτοὺς Ἰησοῦς κατέπαυσεν, οὐκ ἂν περὶ ἄλλης ἐλάλει μετὰ ταῦτα ἡμέρας. ⁹ἄρα ἀπολείπεται σαββατισμὸς τῷ λαῷ τοῦ θεοῦ. ¹⁰ὁ γὰρ εἰσελθὼν εἰς τὴν κατάπαυσιν αὐτοῦ καὶ αὐτὸς κατέπαυσεν ἀπὸ τῶν ἔργων αὐτοῦ ὥσπερ ἀπὸ τῶν ἰδίων ὁ θεός. ¹¹Σπουδάσωμεν οὖν εἰσελθεῖν εἰς ἐκείνην τὴν κατάπαυσιν, ἵνα μὴ ἐν τῷ αὐτῷ τις ὑποδείγματι πέσῃ τῆς ἀπειθείας. ¹²Ζῶν γὰρ ὁ λόγος τοῦ θεοῦ καὶ ἐνεργὴς καὶ τομώτερος ὑπὲρ πᾶσαν μάχαιραν δίστομον καὶ διϊκνούμενος ἄχρι μερισμοῦ ψυχῆς καὶ πνεύματος, ἁρμῶν τε καὶ μυελῶν, καὶ κριτικὸς ἐνθυμήσεων καὶ ἐννοιῶν καρδίας· ¹³καὶ οὐκ ἔστιν κτίσις ἀφανὴς ἐνώπιον αὐτοῦ, πάντα δὲ γυμνὰ καὶ τετραχηλισμένα τοῖς ὀφθαλμοῖς αὐτοῦ, πρὸς ὃν ἡμῖν ὁ λόγος.*

¹Therefore, while the promise of entering his rest remains, let us fear lest any of you be judged to have failed to reach it. ²For good news came to us just as to them; but the message which they heard did not benefit them, because it did not meet with faith in the hearers. ³For we who have believed enter that rest, as he has said, "As I swore in my wrath, 'They shall never enter my rest,'" although his works were finished from the foundation of the world. ⁴For he has somewhere spoken of the seventh day in this way, "And God rested on the seventh day from all his works." ⁵And again in this place he said, "They shall never enter my rest." ⁶Since therefore it remains for some to enter it, and those who formerly received the good news failed to enter because of disobedience, ⁷again he sets a certain day, "Today," saying through David so long afterward, in the words already quoted, "Today, when you hear his voice, do not harden your hearts." ⁸For if Joshua had given them rest, God would not speak later of another day. ⁹So then, there remains a sabbath rest for the people of God; ¹⁰for whoever enters God's rest also ceases from his labors as God did from his. ¹¹Let us therefore strive to enter that rest, that no one fall by the same sort of disobedience. ¹²For the word of God is living and active, sharper than any two-edged sword, piercing to the division of soul and spirit, of joints and marrow, and discerning the thoughts and intentions of the heart. ¹³And before him no creature is hidden, but all are open and laid bare to the eyes of him with whom we have to do.

Chapter 4 continues the argument initiated at the beginning of chapter 3. The promise to enter the "rest" is sure inasmuch as it is God who is its originator. However, the final sharing of each individual in that promised "rest" is conditional; it is based on one's obedience to God's law. And this rule remains in effect within the heir's "house" just as it was within Moses' "house." In order to underscore this reality, the author uses gospel terminology to describe both instances: "For *good news came to us* (*esmen evangelismenoi*; we are evangelized) just as *to them* (they were); but the message which they heard (*ho logos tēs akoēs*; the "word" requiring hearing [obedience]) did not benefit them, because it did not meet with faith (*pistei*) in the hearers (*akousasin*, from the same root as *akoēs*)." (4:2a) This statement is rooted in Paul's teaching in Romans where he speaks of the Old Testament scripture as "gospel" and underscores the obedience to the message of that scripture:

> Paul, a servant of Jesus Christ, called to be an apostle, set apart for the gospel (*evangelion*) of God which he promised beforehand through his prophets in the holy scriptures, (the gospel) concerning his Son, who was descended from David according to the flesh and designated Son of God in power according to the Spirit of holiness by his resurrection from the dead, Jesus Christ our Lord, through whom we have received grace and apostleship to bring about the obedience (*hypakoēn* [from the same root as *akoēs*] of faith (*pisteōs*) for the sake of his name among all the nations, including yourselves who are called to belong to Jesus Christ. (Rom 1:1-6)

This teaching is fleshed out later in these terms;

> But how are men to call upon him in whom they have not believed (*epistevsan*)? And how are they to believe (*pistevsousin*) in him of whom they have never heard (*ēkousan*)? And how are they to hear (*akousōsin*) without a preacher? And how can men preach unless they are sent? As it is written, "How beautiful are the feet of those who preach good news!" But they have not all obeyed (*hypēkousan*) the gospel (*evangelion*); for Isaiah says, "Lord, who has believed (*epistevsen*) *what he has heard* (*akoēs*) from us?" So faith (*pistis*) comes from *what is heard* (*akoēs*), and what is heard (*akoē*) comes by the preaching of Christ. (Rom 10:14-17)

The other side of the coin is that the hearers are to "fear" (Heb 4:1), which is Law terminology. This thought is not strange to the spirit of Romans as Paul writes: "For the law of the Spirit of life in Christ Jesus has set me free from the law of sin and death." (8:2) Such, in turn, is anchored in that "the law is holy, and the commandment is holy and just and good" (7:12).

What seems puzzling in the following verses (Heb 4:3-11) is that the author speaks of the "rest" on the seventh day of creation and then of the "rest" on the sabbath. The question that comes to mind is: What do these two "rests" have to do with the "rest" in Canaan? To answer this, one should start with the investigation of the noun *sabbatismos* (v.9), unique to the entire Bible, which is translated as "sabbath rest" (RSV), or "rest of the seventh day" (JB), or simply "rest" (KJV). However, the ending *–ismos* reflects a manner of behavior as is the case with the rare use of *ioudaismos* (2 Macc 2:21; 8:1; 14:38 [twice]; 4 Macc 4:26; Gal 1:13, 14) whose meaning is "Judaism." This meaning is confirmed by Paul's use of the verb *ioudaizein* (act as a Jew would) in his letter to the Galatians:

> But when I saw that they were not straightforward about the truth of the gospel, I said to Cephas before them all, 'If you, though a Jew, live (*zēs*, from the verb *zēn* [live]) like a Gentile (*ethnikōs*; ethnically) and not like a Jew (*ioudaikōs*; Judaically, Jewishly), how can you compel the Gentiles to *live like Jews* (*ioudaizein*)?' (2:14)

Notice how the last verb *includes* the action of living. This understanding is corroborated by the only other instance of that verb in the Bible: "And many from the peoples of the country *declared themselves Jews* (*ioudaizon*; became Jews [KJV, JB]), for the fear of the Jews had fallen upon them." (Esth 8:17b)

The same phenomenon of verbalization of a noun is found in conjunction with "sabbath," *sabbatizein* (sabbath-ize), whose meaning is "behave as one would on a sabbath":

> So the people *rested* (*esabbatisen*) on the seventh day. (Ex 16:30)

> A man could neither *keep the sabbath* (*sabbatizein*), nor observe the feasts of his fathers, nor so much as confess to be a Jew. (2 Macc 6:6)

And the Lord said to Moses, "On the tenth day of this seventh month is the day of atonement; it shall be for you a time of holy convocation, and you shall afflict yourselves and present an offering by fire to the Lord. And you shall do no work on this same day; for it is a day of atonement, to make atonement for you before the Lord your God. For whoever is not afflicted on this same day shall be cut off from his people. And whoever does any work on this same day, that person I will destroy from among his people. You shall do no work: it is a statute for ever throughout your generations in all your dwellings. It shall be to you a sabbath of solemn rest, and you shall afflict yourselves; on the ninth day of the month beginning at evening, from evening to evening *shall you keep* (*sabbatieite*) your sabbath (*ta sabbata hymōn*; your sabbaths)." (Lev 23:26-32)

And I will devastate the land, so that your enemies who settle in it shall be astonished at it. And I will scatter you among the nations, and I will unsheathe the sword after you; and your land shall be a desolation, and your cities shall be a waste. Then the land shall enjoy its sabbaths as long as it lies desolate, while you are in your enemies' land; then the land shall rest, and enjoy its sabbaths. As long as it lies desolate *it shall have rest* (*sabbatiei*), *the rest which it had* (*esabbatisen*) not in your sabbaths when you dwelt upon it. (Lev 26:32-35)

He [the king of the Chaldeans] took into exile in Babylon those who had escaped from the sword, and they became servants to him and to his sons until the establishment of the kingdom of Persia, to fulfil the word of the Lord by the mouth of Jeremiah, until the land *had enjoyed its sabbaths* (*sabbatisai*). All the days that it lay desolate it kept sabbath (*esabbatisen*), to fulfil seventy years. (2 Chr 36:20-21)

The last passage is an actualization of Leviticus 26:32-35. So it is the two passages of Leviticus that are important for our discussion. Both use the verb *sabbatizein* in conjunction with atonement for the people's sins, either through offering of sacrifices or through punishment by exile. The purpose of the exile is to have the land of the promise experience a sabbath rest from the people's sins that polluted it and rendered it no longer a property where the Lord's will is done. This thought is definitely on the mind of the writer of Leviticus since the previous chapter 25 is dedicated to the sabbatical year and especially the jubilee year (seven sabbaths of years) during which the land is "liberated" and returns to the original people to whom it was allocated by God himself in the Book of Joshua. One can safely surmise that the author of Hebrews had all the preceding in mind, especially when one considers that he ends his discussion by underscoring that the "word" of God is a word of judgment over any disobedience perpetrated in the land of rest (Heb 4:11-13).

Keeping this in mind, the hearers can follow why and how the author is bringing into the picture the quotation from Genesis 2:2 regarding God's rest on the seventh day (Heb 4:4, 10). The entire argument of 3:7-4:3 revolves around the earth of the promise as a place of rest (*katapavsin*) and, more specifically, around a rest that was denied (3:11, 18; 4:5) to the fathers (3:9) because they did not hearken to God's voice (3:7b, 15; 4:7b). This statement appears on the lips of David, the assumed author of Psalms (4:7), and includes a cautioning not to follow in the fathers' footsteps: "Today, when you hear his voice, do not harden your hearts." Since David enters the scriptural scene later than Moses and Joshua, then this warning is made to David's contemporaries and the following generations of hearers. If these hearers follow the rulings of God's voice, then they will become God's people (4:9) and he their God (Jer 24:7; 31:33; 32:38; Ezek 11:20; 14:11; 37:27) under the leadership of the new David (vv.24-26), the heir Jesus, and, as such, they will be entitled to the "rest." Still, since the heir's heritage is the *oikoumenē*, that is, the Roman empire encompassing all nations residing therein, the author appeals to scripture to show that the rest (*katapavsin*) was on God's mind "from the foundation of the world" (Heb 4:3) and thus it concerns every "human being" (*'adam*): "And God rested (*katepavsen*, from the same root as *katapavsin*) on the seventh day from all his works." (v.4; Gen 2:2). If the author of the Pentateuch shies from referring openly to the seventh day as sabbath, it is out of deference to the fact that the sabbath is an institution of the Mosaic law. However, the indirect link between the two is detectable in the Hebrew since the noun *šabbat* (sabbath) and the verb *šabat* (rest) are from the same root. The intended connection between the two is evident in the LXX that uses similar phraseology to speak of the rest of God on the seventh day and that of the people on the sabbath as seventh day. Consider the following:

> And on the seventh day God finished his work (Greek *erga* [plural]; Hebrew *mela'kah*) which he had done, and he rested (Greek *katepavsen*; Hebrew *šabat*) on the seventh day from all his work (Greek *ergon* [singular]; Hebrew *mela'kah*) which he had done. So God blessed the seventh day and hallowed it, because on it God rested (Greek *katepavsen*; Hebrew *šabat*) from all his work (Greek *ergōn* [plural]; Hebrew *mela'kah*) which he had done in creation. (Gen 2:2-3)

> Six days shall work (Greek *erga* [plural]; Hebrew *mela'kah*) be done, but on the seventh day you shall have a holy sabbath (Greek *sabbata* [plural]; Hebrew *šabbat*) of solemn rest (Greek *katapavsis*; Hebrew *šabbaton*) to the Lord; whoever does any work (Greek *ergon* [singular]; Hebrew *mela'kah*) on it shall be put to death; you shall kindle no fire in all your habitations on the sabbath (Greek *sabbatōn*; Hebrew *šabbat*) day. (Ex 35:2-3)

Two remarks are in order. The first one is that, in speaking of the sabbath, LXX Exodus uses first the plural *erga* (works) followed by the singular *ergon* (work) to render the original Hebrew singular *mela'kah* in both cases, which is precisely the case in Genesis. This can hardly be happenstance. The other feature of the Exodus passage pertinent to our discussion is that it contains the first occurrence of the noun *katapavsis* (rest) in scripture. So the assertion of the author of Hebrews that God had in mind the "rest" of Psalm 95:11 (Heb 3:11, 18; 4:3, 5) is warranted. The following instance of that noun in the Law (Genesis through Deuteronomy) refers to the impending entrance into Canaan: "for you have not as yet come to the rest (*katapavsin*) and to the inheritance which the Lord your God gives you. But when you go over the Jordan, and live in the land which the Lord your God gives you to inherit, and when he *gives you rest* (*katapavsei* [verb]) from all your enemies round about, so that you live in safety." (Deut 12:9-10) In the Pentateuch, the close relationship between God's rest on the seventh day, i.e., the rest on the sabbath, and the rest in the earth of inheritance after the exodus from Egypt is at clearest in the two versions of the Decalogue:

> Remember the sabbath day, to keep it holy. Six days you shall labor, and do all your work; but the seventh day is a sabbath to the Lord your God; in it you shall not do any work, you, or your son, or your daughter, your manservant, or your maidservant, or your cattle, or the sojourner who is within your gates; for in six days the Lord made heaven and earth, the sea, and all that is in them, and rested the seventh day; therefore the Lord blessed the sabbath day and hallowed it. (Ex 20:8-11)

> Observe the sabbath day, to keep it holy, as the Lord your God commanded you. Six days you shall labor, and do all your work; but the seventh day is a sabbath to the Lord your God; in it

you shall not do any work, you, or your son, or your daughter, or your manservant, or your maidservant, or your ox, or your ass, or any of your cattle, or the sojourner who is within your gates, that your manservant and your maidservant may rest as well as you. You shall remember that you were a servant in the land of Egypt, and the Lord your God brought you out thence with a mighty hand and an outstretched arm; therefore the Lord your God commanded you to keep the sabbath day. (Deut 5:12-15)

The intention of the interrelationship is obvious. The people are to follow the example of God and rest from work on the sabbath. God rests from his work in order to deliver his *torah*; the people rest from their "work" (doings) to hear that *torah* in order to "do" it, that is, obey its instruction, during their working days. This is corroborated by the injunction at the start of the Decalogue in Deuteronomy: "Hear, O Israel, the statutes and the ordinances which I speak in your hearing this day, and you shall learn them and be careful to do them." (5:1) In turn, it is by "doing" God's will on their "working" days that the people are guaranteed "rest" in the earth of promise:

> Now this is the commandment, the statutes and the ordinances which the Lord your God commanded me to teach you, that you may do them in the land to which you are going over, to possess (Hebrew "inherit") it; that you may fear the Lord you God, you and your son and your son's son, by keeping all his statutes and his commandments, which I command you, all the days of your life; and that your days may be prolonged. Hear therefore, O Israel, and be careful to do them; that it may go well with you, and that you may multiply greatly, as the Lord, the God of your fathers, has promised you, in a land flowing with milk and honey. (6:1-3)

The author of Hebrews then proceeds to issue a strong caveat to his hearers similar to that of Paul in Galatians: the inheritance and the "rest" are conditional on fulfilling the divine will. To emphasize this, he moves to the scriptural book following the Law, the Book of Joshua: "For if Joshua had given them rest, God would not speak later of another day." (Heb 4:8) The ingeniousness of this verse lies in that it plays on different levels. First, it shows, by the witness of scripture itself, that the people did not attain the promised rest after Joshua's death because they forsook the Lord:

> When Joshua dismissed the people, the people of Israel went each to his inheritance to take possession of the land. And the people served the Lord all the days of Joshua, and all the days of the elders who outlived Joshua, who had seen all the great work which the Lord had done for Israel. And Joshua the son of Nun, the servant of the Lord, died at the age of one hundred and ten years. And they buried him within the bounds of his inheritance in Timnath-heres, in the hill country of Ephraim, north of the mountain of Gaash. And all that generation also were gathered to their fathers; and there arose another generation after them, who did not know the Lord or the work which he had done for Israel. And the people of Israel did what was evil in the sight of the Lord and served the Baals; and they forsook the Lord, the God of their fathers, who had brought them out of the land of Egypt; they went after other gods, from among the gods of the peoples who were round about them, and bowed down to them; and they provoked the Lord to anger. They forsook the Lord, and served the Baals and the Ashtaroth. So the anger of the Lord was kindled against Israel, and he gave them over to plunderers, who plundered them; and he sold them into the power of their enemies round about, so that they could no longer withstand their enemies. Whenever they marched out, the hand of the Lord was against them for evil, as the Lord had warned, and as the Lord had sworn to them; and they were in sore straits. (Judg 2:6-15)

This allows the author to explain why God, in his mercy, spoke later through David the Psalmist, of "another day," thus giving a new chance to anyone who would not "harden his heart as in the rebellion, on the day of testing in the wilderness" (Heb 3:7b-8). Finally, the Greek *Iēsous* (Jesus) for the Hebrew *yehošuaʻ* (Joshua) paves the way for the author to forewarn his hearers that even Jesus Christ would not save them, in spite of their being "the house of Christ" (3:6) and "the people of God" (4:9), if they imitate the members of the "house of Moses" (3:2, 5). "Let us therefore," he urges them, "strive to enter that rest, that no one fall by the same sort of disobedience" (4:11). The reason is that "the word of God," that is the Old Testament scripture, is abidingly "living" and still "active" (*energēs*; effective, at work) and carries God's judgment (v.12) just as Paul's gospel does. The adjective *kritikos* (v.13), translated as "discerning," is from the same root as the verb *krinei* (judges). Paul uses this when speaking about the divine judgment of all according to "my gospel" that is "the gospel of God, which he promised beforehand through his prophets in the holy scriptures" (Rom 1:1-2). Compare Hebrews 4:12-13 with Romans 2:13-16:

> For the word of God is living and active, sharper than any two-edged sword, piercing to the division of soul and spirit, of joints and marrow, and discerning the thoughts and intentions of the heart. And before him no creature is hidden, but all are open and laid bare to the eyes of him with whom we have to do. (Hebrews)

> For it is not the hearers of the law who are righteous before God, *but the doers of the law who will be justified*. When Gentiles who have not the law *do by nature what the law requires*, they are a law to themselves, even though they do not have the law. They show that *what the law requires* is written on their hearts, while their conscience also bears witness and their conflicting thoughts accuse

or perhaps excuse them on that day when, according to my gospel, God judges (*krinei*) the *secrets of men* by Christ Jesus. (Romans)

This central teaching concerning our accountability to God in the matter of doing his will expressed in his commandments is captured by the author on the literary level. In the original Greek, Hebrews 4:12-13 is bracketed by the noun *logos* (word). KJV and RSV mask this feature of accountability by translating the concluding phrase *pros hon hēmin ho logos* into "with whom we have to do." JB is closer when it renders it as "to whom we must give account of ourselves." Had JB translated also *ho logos tou Theou* (the word of God) at the beginning of v.12 as "the account of God," it would have fully captured the word play of the original. Indeed, the scriptural teaching to which the phrase "word of God" refers is expressed through his actual "words" as we hear in Jeremiah:

> The *words* of Jeremiah, the son of Hilkiah, of the priests who were in Anathoth in the land of Benjamin, to whom the *word* of the Lord came ... Then the Lord put forth his hand and touched my mouth; and the Lord said to me, "Behold, I have put *my words* in your mouth." (1:1-2a, 9)
>
> And the Lord said to me, "Faithless Israel has shown herself less guilty than false Judah. Go, and proclaim *these words* toward the north, and say..." (3:11-12)
>
> Therefore thus says the Lord, the God of hosts: "Because they have spoken this word, behold, I am making *my words* in your mouth a fire and this people wood, and the fire shall devour them." (5:14)
>
> Hear, O earth; behold, I am bringing evil upon this people, the fruit of their devices, because they have not given heed to *my words*; and as for *my law*, they have rejected it. (6:19)

Chapter 4

> Thus says the Lord: Stand in the court of the Lord's house, and speak to all the cities of Judah which come to worship in the house of the Lord *all the words that I command you to speak* to them; do not hold back *a (one) word*. (26:2)

> In the fourth year of Jehoiakim the son of Josiah, king of Judah, this word came to Jeremiah from the Lord: "Take a scroll and write on it *all the words that I have spoken to you* against Israel and Judah and all the nations, from the day I spoke to you, from the days of Josiah until today." (36:1-2)

The many words form an "account," which corresponds perfectly with scripture since the delivery of the divine words, embedded in a story, form an "account." One can find corroboration of this in Luke-Acts where the author refers to his Gospel as a 'narrative" (*diēgēsin*; Lk 1:1) addressed to Theophilus (v.3), and later he refers to that "narrative" as *logos* (word): "In the first book (*logon*; word), O Theophilus, I have dealt with all that Jesus began to do and teach." (Acts 1:1) In this case, the "account" is the teaching of a senior toward a junior. On the other hand, the same noun "account" may refer to "an explanatory statement of conduct to a superior" as in "give or render account" (of one's actions). Thus, the *logos* of God will require equally a *logos* from those who were the recipients of that word (Heb 4:12-13). What is significant for our case here is that Luke uses this same phraseology in one of his parables:

> There was a rich man who had a steward, and charges were brought to him that this man was wasting his goods. And he called him and said to him, "What is this that I hear about you? Turn in (*apodos*, from the verb *apodidōmi*) the account (*logon*) of your stewardship, for you can no longer be steward." (Lk 16:1-2, in both KJV and RSV)

Listening closely to the verse dealing with the divine judgment, one will soon discover another function to the choice of Genesis 2-3: "And before him no creature (*ktisis*; creation) is hidden, but all are open (*gymna*; naked) and laid bare (*tetrakhēlismena*; held down by the neck, with the neck held stretched [with the intention of breaking or axing it]) to the eyes of him with whom we have to do (*hēmin ho logos*; we must give account for ourselves)." (Heb 4:13) The only other scriptural instance where nakedness is associated with divine judgment occurs in Genesis 3:

> And the man and his wife were both naked (*gymnoi*), and were not ashamed ... Then the eyes of both were opened, and they knew that they were naked (*gymnoi*); and they sewed fig leaves together and made themselves aprons. And they heard the sound of the Lord God walking in the garden in the cool of the day, and the man and his wife hid themselves from the presence of the Lord God among the trees of the garden. But the Lord God called to the man, and said to him, "Where are you?" And he said, "I heard the sound of thee in the garden, and I was afraid, because I was naked (*gymnos*); and I hid myself." He said, "Who told you that you were naked (*gymnos*)? Have you eaten of the tree of which I commanded you not to eat?" (Gen 2:25; 3:7-11)

In the original Hebrew, the choice of *gymna* (naked) in Hebrews 4:13 brings to mind an even stronger and more direct way the conclusion we arrived at, namely, that every human being (*'adam*) will be brought to judgment for one's own actions. Still, the story of the divine judgment in Genesis aptly fits the wording of Hebrews in that "the word (commandment) of God" (Gen 2:17; see Heb 4:12) is the basis of the "account" Adam had to render (Gen 3:7-11) and that "all" will have to render (Heb 4:13). The connotation of universal judgment is further enhanced through the use of the verb *trakhēlizomai*, a unique instance in the entire Bible. This verb reflects death by beheading through axing off at the neck, which is tantamount to capital punishment. The metaphoric equation between "life" and "neck"—as in risking one's neck for someone else's sake—is common to most languages. In the Pauline corpus, one encounters this metaphor in the letter to the Romans: "Greet Prisca and Aquila, my fellow workers in Christ Jesus, who risked (*hypethēkan*; laid down) their necks (*ton heavtōn trakhēlon* [neck]) for my life, to whom not only I but also all the churches of the Gentiles give thanks." (Rom 16:3-4)

Chapter 5

Vv. 4:14-16 ¹⁴Ἔχοντες οὖν ἀρχιερέα μέγαν διεληλυθότα τοὺς οὐρανούς, Ἰησοῦν τὸν υἱὸν τοῦ θεοῦ, κρατῶμεν τῆς ὁμολογίας. ¹⁵οὐ γὰρ ἔχομεν ἀρχιερέα μὴ δυνάμενον συμπαθῆσαι ταῖς ἀσθενείαις ἡμῶν, πεπειρασμένον δὲ κατὰ πάντα καθ᾽ ὁμοιότητα χωρὶς ἁμαρτίας. ¹⁶προσερχώμεθα οὖν μετὰ παρρησίας τῷ θρόνῳ τῆς χάριτος, ἵνα λάβωμεν ἔλεος καὶ χάριν εὕρωμεν εἰς εὔκαιρον βοήθειαν.

¹⁴Since then we have a great high priest who has passed through the heavens, Jesus, the Son of God, let us hold fast our confession. ¹⁵For we have not a high priest who is unable to sympathize with our weaknesses, but one who in every respect has been tempted as we are, yet without sin. ¹⁶Let us then with confidence draw near to the throne of grace, that we may receive mercy and find grace to help in time of need.

Having established the likeness between Jesus Christ and Moses, the author moves to the likeness between Jesus and Aaron. The reason is obvious. Moses, the lawgiver, is a person totally of the past; he survives as a "book." Aaron, on the other hand, is functionally perennial in his progeny, the priests who are "sons of Aaron"[1] and, more specifically, the high priests in every generation whose function is to atone for the sins of the people whenever they contravene Moses' statutes and commandments. This is precisely what was needed since Joshua, the first Jesus, was able to secure the "rest" in the earth of inheritance only during his lifetime. Now that the hearers are granted the "rest" of the heavenly Jerusalem through the Jesus of "these last days" (Heb 1:2), falling away from that calling would mean eternal damnation outside the walls of that city (Is 66:24) where the "throne of grace" (Heb 4:16a) lies. Hence, and in

---

[1] Lev 1:7-8; 7:32-33; 21:1; Num 10:8; 2 Chr 13:9, 10; 26:18; 29:21; 31:19; 36:14.

order to avoid such a calamity, they are exhorted to "hold fast our confession" (v.14) whose "apostle and high priest" is that same Jesus (3:1) and "draw near with confidence to the throne of grace" (4:16a). Still, as is the case of the assuredness guaranteed by the gospel message, nothing is all set until judgment day. That is why the author speaks of asking God's "help in time of need" (v.16b). The time of need is obviously when one is overtaken by temptation, which is to be expected since Jesus himself "has been tempted in every respect as we are." However, he did not succumb to the sin of revolt and disobedience (v.15): "He was oppressed, and he was afflicted, yet he opened not his mouth; like a lamb that is led to the slaughter, and like a sheep that before its shearers is dumb, so he opened not his mouth." (Is 53:7) That is why "He has no need, like those high priests, to offer sacrifices daily, first for his own sins and then for those of the people." (Heb 7:27a)

The sinlessness of Jesus may not be understood as an "essential" (eternal) feature, as is done in classical theology, but rather in the sense that he did not commit the sin of disobedience *when he was tempted*. Understanding his sinlessness as being eternal would contradict the message underscoring all his temptations, especially at the beginning (Mt 4:1-11; Mk 1:12-13; Lk 4:1-13) and end (Mt 26:36-46; Mk 14:32-42; Lk 22:39-46) of his life. The temptations at the end of his life are more pertinent for two reasons. First, just as in Hebrews 4:16, Jesus summons his disciples to "pray in order not to succumb to (fall into) the temptation" (Mt 26:41; Mk 14:38, 46; Lk 22:40); secondly, the realism of Jesus' temptation is underscored in many ancient manuscripts: "And there appeared an angel unto him from heaven, strengthening him. And being *in an agony* he prayed *more earnestly*; and his sweat was as it were great drops of blood falling down to the ground." (Lk 22:43-44) At any rate, were he "essentially" sinless, his being tempted would have been fake and, more importantly, he would not "have been tempted in every respect as we are," nor would he have been able "to sympathize with our weaknesses" (Heb 4:15). The contrast between him and us lies in our disobedience and his unconditional submission to the will of his God and Father.[2]

Vv. 5:1-10 ¹Πᾶς γὰρ ἀρχιερεὺς ἐξ ἀνθρώπων λαμβανόμενος ὑπὲρ ἀνθρώπων καθίσταται τὰ πρὸς τὸν θεόν, ἵνα προσφέρῃ δῶρά τε καὶ θυσίας ὑπὲρ ἁμαρτιῶν, ²μετριοπαθεῖν δυνάμενος τοῖς ἀγνοοῦσιν καὶ πλανωμένοις, ἐπεὶ καὶ αὐτὸς περίκειται ἀσθένειαν ³καὶ δι' αὐτὴν ὀφείλει, καθὼς περὶ τοῦ λαοῦ, οὕτως καὶ περὶ αὐτοῦ προσφέρειν περὶ ἁμαρτιῶν. ⁴καὶ οὐχ ἑαυτῷ τις λαμβάνει τὴν τιμὴν ἀλλὰ καλούμενος ὑπὸ τοῦ θεοῦ καθώσπερ καὶ Ἀαρών. ⁵οὕτως καὶ ὁ Χριστὸς οὐχ ἑαυτὸν ἐδόξασεν γενηθῆναι ἀρχιερέα ἀλλ' ὁ λαλήσας πρὸς αὐτόν· υἱός μου εἶ σύ, ἐγὼ σήμερον γεγέννηκά σε· ⁶καθὼς καὶ ἐν ἑτέρῳ λέγει· σὺ ἱερεὺς εἰς τὸν αἰῶνα κατὰ τὴν τάξιν Μελχισέδεκ, ⁷ὃς ἐν ταῖς ἡμέραις τῆς σαρκὸς αὐτοῦ δεήσεις τε καὶ ἱκετηρίας πρὸς τὸν δυνάμενον σῴζειν αὐτὸν ἐκ θανάτου μετὰ κραυγῆς ἰσχυρᾶς καὶ δακρύων προσενέγκας καὶ εἰσακουσθεὶς ἀπὸ τῆς εὐλαβείας, ⁸καίπερ ὢν υἱός, ἔμαθεν ἀφ' ὧν ἔπαθεν τὴν ὑπακοήν, ⁹καὶ τελειωθεὶς ἐγένετο πᾶσιν τοῖς ὑπακούουσιν αὐτῷ αἴτιος σωτηρίας αἰωνίου, ¹⁰προσαγορευθεὶς ὑπὸ τοῦ θεοῦ ἀρχιερεὺς κατὰ τὴν τάξιν Μελχισέδεκ.

¹For every high priest chosen from among men is appointed to act on behalf of men in relation to God, to offer gifts and sacrifices for sins. ²He can deal gently with the ignorant and wayward, since he himself is beset with weakness. ³Because of this he is bound to offer sacrifice for his own sins as well as for those of the people. ⁴And one does not take the honor upon himself, but he is called by God, just as Aaron was. ⁵So also Christ did not exalt himself to be made a high priest, but was appointed by him who said to him, "Thou art my Son, today I

---

[2] See my comments on 2 Cor 1:3-7 in *C-2Cor*.

> have begotten thee"; ⁶*as he says also in another place, "Thou art a priest for ever, after the order of Melchizedek." ⁷In the days of his flesh, Jesus offered up prayers and supplications, with loud cries and tears, to him who was able to save him from death, and he was heard for his godly fear. ⁸Although he was a Son, he learned obedience through what he suffered; ⁹and being made perfect he became the source of eternal salvation to all who obey him, ¹⁰being designated by God a high priest after the order of Melchizedek.*

Such understanding of the temptations of Jesus is confirmed in 5:1-6 where he is presented in parallel to "every high priest chosen from among men" (v.1) who "can deal gently with the ignorant and wayward, since (*epei kai*; because also) he himself is beset with weakness" (v.2). Indeed, the latter statement is a rephrasing of 4:15a: "For we have not a high priest who is unable to sympathize with our weaknesses." Notice how the element that links the two statements is "weakness." Furthermore and more importantly, the parallelism between Aaron and Christ lies in that neither "exalted (*edoxasen*; glorified) himself to be made a high priest" (5:5a), but rather both were assigned to that position of honor by God (v.4) and not because of some value inherent in them. The "today" of Psalm 2:7 (Heb 5:5b) is not an "eternal today," but a given day, the day of enthronement during which time one *is born as*, and therefore *becomes*, "son of God." It is as much a given and thus functional "today" as the "today" of Psalm 95:7 (Heb 3:7a, 13, 15; 4:7). The stress on the *accession* to the glory at a given moment is underscored by the author's reference to Psalm 110:4, which immediately follows: "Thou art a priest for ever, after the order of Melchizedek." (Heb 5:6) This address takes effect in conjunction with "the Lord's saying to my lord: 'Sit at my right hand, till I make your enemies your footstool'" (Ps 110:1).

Consequently, one should not understand "in the days of his flesh" (Heb 5:7) within the Platonic premise of "incarnation," but rather in the sense of "flesh" being reflective of "weakness," a word that was just used twice in conjunction with "temptation." This is corroborated in the pericopes dealing with the last temptation of Jesus in the Gospel narratives: "Watch and pray that you may not enter into temptation; the spirit indeed is willing, but the flesh is weak." (Mt 26:41; Mk 14:38) That the author of Hebrews had that scenario in mind is confirmed by the entirety of his statement in 5:7: "In the days of his flesh, Jesus offered up prayers and supplications, with loud cries and tears, to him who was able to save him from death, and he was heard for his godly fear." And again, it is not only the element of obedience that is brought to the fore, but that Jesus learned such obedience through the suffering he had to endure "although he was a Son" (v.8). This obedience in turn allowed him to "be made perfect" and "*become* the source of eternal salvation to all who obey him," that is to say, he was found worthy of his assignment by God as a high priest after the order of Melchizedek (v.9). This is the thesis of Philippians 2:5-11, a passage showed earlier to be on the author's mind. In other words, one's assignment entails a mission, and upon completion, one is ultimately honored; however, such is not *harpagmon* (a thing to be grasped, hold unto as one's possession; Phil 2:6).[3] In Philippians, Christ is ultimately spoken of as an example of obedience for the hearers to follow. Here also in Hebrews, the author uses Christ's obedience as an example for his addressees to emulate:

> Therefore, my beloved, as you have always *obeyed*, so now, not only as in my presence but much more in my absence, work out

---

[3] See my comments in *C-Phil* 115-7.

your own *salvation* with fear and trembling; for God is at work in you, both to will and to work for his good pleasure. (Phil 2:12-13)

... and being made perfect he became the source of eternal *salvation* to all who *obey* him ... (Heb 5:9)

Chapter 6

Vv. 5:11-14 *¹¹Περὶ οὗ πολὺς ἡμῖν ὁ λόγος καὶ δυσερμήνευτος λέγειν, ἐπεὶ νωθροὶ γεγόνατε ταῖς ἀκοαῖς. ¹²καὶ γὰρ ὀφείλοντες εἶναι διδάσκαλοι διὰ τὸν χρόνον, πάλιν χρείαν ἔχετε τοῦ διδάσκειν ὑμᾶς τινὰ τὰ στοιχεῖα τῆς ἀρχῆς τῶν λογίων τοῦ θεοῦ καὶ γεγόνατε χρείαν ἔχοντες γάλακτος [καὶ] οὐ στερεᾶς τροφῆς. ¹³πᾶς γὰρ ὁ μετέχων γάλακτος ἄπειρος λόγου δικαιοσύνης, νήπιος γάρ ἐστιν· ¹⁴τελείων δέ ἐστιν ἡ στερεὰ τροφή, τῶν διὰ τὴν ἕξιν τὰ αἰσθητήρια γεγυμνασμένα ἐχόντων πρὸς διάκρισιν καλοῦ τε καὶ κακοῦ.*

Vv. 6:1-12 *¹Διὸ ἀφέντες τὸν τῆς ἀρχῆς τοῦ Χριστοῦ λόγον ἐπὶ τὴν τελειότητα φερώμεθα, μὴ πάλιν θεμέλιον καταβαλλόμενοι μετανοίας ἀπὸ νεκρῶν ἔργων καὶ πίστεως ἐπὶ θεόν, ²βαπτισμῶν διδαχῆς ἐπιθέσεώς τε χειρῶν, ἀναστάσεώς τε νεκρῶν καὶ κρίματος αἰωνίου. ³καὶ τοῦτο ποιήσομεν, ἐάνπερ ἐπιτρέπῃ ὁ θεός. ⁴Ἀδύνατον γὰρ τοὺς ἅπαξ φωτισθέντας, γευσαμένους τε τῆς δωρεᾶς τῆς ἐπουρανίου καὶ μετόχους γενηθέντας πνεύματος ἁγίου ⁵καὶ καλὸν γευσαμένους θεοῦ ῥῆμα δυνάμεις τε μέλλοντος αἰῶνος ⁶καὶ παραπεσόντας, πάλιν ἀνακαινίζειν εἰς μετάνοιαν, ἀνασταυροῦντας ἑαυτοῖς τὸν υἱὸν τοῦ θεοῦ καὶ παραδειγματίζοντας. ⁷γῆ γὰρ ἡ πιοῦσα τὸν ἐπ᾽ αὐτῆς ἐρχόμενον πολλάκις ὑετὸν καὶ τίκτουσα βοτάνην εὔθετον ἐκείνοις δι᾽ οὓς καὶ γεωργεῖται, μεταλαμβάνει εὐλογίας ἀπὸ τοῦ θεοῦ· ⁸ἐκφέρουσα δὲ ἀκάνθας καὶ τριβόλους, ἀδόκιμος καὶ κατάρας ἐγγύς, ἧς τὸ τέλος εἰς καῦσιν. ⁹Πεπείσμεθα δὲ περὶ ὑμῶν, ἀγαπητοί, τὰ κρείσσονα καὶ ἐχόμενα σωτηρίας, εἰ καὶ οὕτως λαλοῦμεν. ¹⁰οὐ γὰρ ἄδικος ὁ θεὸς ἐπιλαθέσθαι τοῦ ἔργου ὑμῶν καὶ τῆς ἀγάπης ἧς ἐνεδείξασθε εἰς τὸ ὄνομα αὐτοῦ, διακονήσαντες τοῖς ἁγίοις καὶ διακονοῦντες. ¹¹ἐπιθυμοῦμεν δὲ ἕκαστον ὑμῶν τὴν αὐτὴν ἐνδείκνυσθαι σπουδὴν πρὸς τὴν πληροφορίαν τῆς ἐλπίδος ἄχρι τέλους, ¹²ἵνα μὴ νωθροὶ γένησθε, μιμηταὶ δὲ τῶν διὰ πίστεως καὶ μακροθυμίας κληρονομούντων τὰς ἐπαγγελίας.*

5:11-14 *¹¹About this we have much to say which is hard to explain, since you have become dull of hearing. ¹²For though by* this time you ought to be teachers, you need some one to teach you again the first principles of God's word. You need milk, not solid food; *¹³for every one who lives on milk is unskilled in the word of righteousness, for he is a child. ¹⁴But solid food is for the mature, for those who have their faculties trained by practice to distinguish good from evil.*

6:1-12 *¹Therefore let us leave the elementary doctrine of Christ and go on to maturity, not laying again a foundation of repentance from dead works and of faith toward God, ²with instruction about ablutions, the laying on of hands, the resurrection of the dead, and eternal judgment. ³And this we will do if God permits. ⁴For it is impossible to restore again to repentance those who have once been enlightened, who have tasted the heavenly gift, and have become partakers of the Holy Spirit, ⁵and have tasted the goodness of the word of God and the powers of the age to come, ⁶if they then commit apostasy, since they crucify the Son of God on their own account and hold him up to contempt. ⁷For land which has drunk the rain that often falls upon it, and brings forth vegetation useful to those for whose sake it is cultivated, receives a blessing from God. ⁸But if it bears thorns and thistles, it is worthless and near to being cursed; its end is to be burned. ⁹Though we speak thus, yet in your case, beloved, we feel sure of better things that belong to salvation. ¹⁰For God is not so unjust as to overlook your work and the love which you showed for his sake in serving the saints, as you still do. ¹¹And we desire each one of you to show the same earnestness in realizing the full assurance of hope until the end, ¹²so that you may not be sluggish, but imitators of those who through faith and patience inherit the promises.*

At this point the author explains what all the preceding entails, which in the Pauline corpus is always a matter of behavior rather than a mental belief in God or topics related to him. This is evident from the last verses of chapter 5. The phraseology of teaching, discerning (distinguishing), and being a child (*nēpios*; babe), in juxtaposition to that of maturity, and also that of milk to solid food, is patterned after 1 Corinthians 2-3:

> Yet among the mature (*teleiois*) we do impart wisdom, although it is not a wisdom of this age or of the rulers of this age, who are doomed to pass away … And we impart this in words not taught (*didaktois*; from the verb *didaskein*) by human wisdom but taught (*didaktois*) by the Spirit, interpreting spiritual truths to those who possess the Spirit. The unspiritual man does not receive the gifts of the Spirit of God, for they are folly to him, and he is not able to understand them because they are spiritually discerned (*synkrinontes*; from the same root as *diakrisin*) … But I, brethren, could not address you as spiritual men, but as men of the flesh, as babes (*nēpiois*) in Christ. I fed you with milk, not solid food; for you were not ready for it. (2:6, 13-14; 3:1-2)

In Corinthians the language is metaphorical since babes *cannot* understand; in Hebrews the addressees *are unwilling* to do so (5:11b). In both cases, the writer's intention is to shame the recipients of the letter. Furthermore, the "mature" are not those whose faculties are challenged through exercise in higher levels of mental perception of ethics à la Aristotle. Instead, those faculties are to be trained (*gegymnasmena*)—as one would train in a gymnasium through repeated practice—to discern between good and evil (v.14) in order *to do* the good rather than the evil. This, after all, is the consistent message of the entire scripture starting with Genesis 2-3 where the only test that Adam was supposed to pass was linked to the tree of the knowledge of good and evil. Adam and Eve were fooled into believing that they could become like God, discerning between good and evil, when in reality, God's commandment not to do so (2:17) was the "good"

Adam was supposed to *practice*. In other words, it is God alone who decides what is "good." Human beings, on the other hand, will have to give account to God whether or not they have done that "good."

The Greek *gegymnasmena* is from the root *gymnos* (naked). This makes sense since the athletes take off their clothing in order to train or compete. The gymnasium (*gymnasion*) is essentially a place where one is bare; hence the verb *gymnazein* (train) was coined accordingly. Its choice here is dictated by the earlier use of *gymna* (naked; laid bare), the state all human beings will be in on judgment day (Heb 4:13). So the author is encouraging his hearers to practice being in that state in order not to be caught unaware on that day. This corresponds to Paul's cautioning in 1 Thessalonians, advice that is taken up by the Gospels' authors:

> So then let us not sleep, as others do, but let us keep awake (*grēgorōmen*) and be sober. For those who sleep sleep at night, and those who get drunk are drunk at night. But, since we belong to the day, let us be sober, and put on the breastplate of faith and love, and for a helmet the hope of salvation. For God has not destined us for wrath, but to obtain salvation through our Lord Jesus Christ, who died for us so that whether we wake or sleep we might live with him. Therefore encourage one another and build one another up, just as you are doing. (1 Thess 5:6-11)[1]

The interconnection of Hebrews 4:12-13 and 5:11-13 is very clear in the original. Because scripture, "the word of God" (*ho logos tou Theou*; 4:12), will judge all human beings, both the apostle and his addressees will have to "render account" (*hēmin ho logos*; v.13). For that reason, the apostle is "accountable"

---

[1] See Mt 24:42-43; 25:13; 26:41; Mk 13:32-36; 14:38 where the same verb *grēgorein* occurs, often translated as "watch, be watchful."

(*hēmin ho logos*) for insuring that the teaching be "much (repeatedly)" (*polys*) "conveyed (said)" (*legein*) in spite of it being "hard to explain" (*dysermēnevtos*) (5:11a). Notice how the apostolic duty and the inevitability of the judgment are rendered through the same phrase *hēmin ho logos*, and how both find their rationale in *ho logos tou Theou*. However, time is of the essence. With every day that goes by, one is nearer to the judgment, as Paul writes in Romans: "Besides this you know what hour it is, how it is full time now for you to wake from sleep. For salvation is nearer to us now than when we first believed; the night is far gone, the day is at hand. Let us then cast off *the works of darkness* and put on the armor of light." (13:11-12)

So the author is urging his hearers to move beyond the basics, beginning with the *dead works*, from which one is supposed to have repented (*metanoias*) and believed (*pisteōs*) in God (Heb 6:1), and ending with the judgment beyond the resurrection of the dead (v.2). The ultimate aim of the gospel preaching is precisely repentance from "dead works": "Now after John was arrested, Jesus came into Galilee, preaching the gospel of God, and saying, 'The time is fulfilled, and the kingdom of God is at hand; repent (*metanoeite*), and believe (*pistevete*) in the gospel.'" (Mk 1:14-15) The author increases the pressure on his addressees by stating that, in practicality, it is impossible (Heb 6:4), in the sense of implausible, for someone who has already "tasted" the "good utterance (*rhēma*) of God" (6:5) and its effects (vv.4-5) to "fall" (v.6)[2] away "from grace," as Paul writes in Galatians (5:4), and undergo another repentance (Heb 6:6 in Greek; v.4 RSV).[3] By falling from the grace brought about by the gospel, one would have committed desertion (Gal 1:6) and

---

[2] RSV has "commit apostasy."
[3] This is due to the difference in syntax between the two languages.

thus the sin of high treason.[4] In other words, that person would have joined the enemy in the act of crucifying the Son of God, that is to say, holding him up to contempt and utter shame (Heb 6:6), instead of acknowledging his crucifixion as a point of honor (Gal 6:14) and accepting to join him on the cross (2:20) by crucifying, for his sake, one's own passions and desires (5:24).

To back up his argument the author appeals to Deuteronomy and its language of blessing and curse in chapter 28 (Heb 6:7-8) which, in turn, rejoins Paul's argument in Galatians 3:6-14 where we hear of the curse from which we were saved through the blessing promised to Abraham. The link with Galatians will be sealed a few verses later when the author brings into the picture the divine blessing bestowed on Abraham (Heb 6:13-14).

Throughout Hebrews, the author repeatedly dips into the rich inventory of the Pauline corpus. In vv. 7 and 8, he uses the imagery of the field from 1 Corinthians to refer to curse versus blessing:

> What then is Apollos? What is Paul? Servants through whom you believed, as the Lord assigned to each. I planted, Apollos watered, but God gave the growth. So neither he who plants nor he who *waters* is anything, but only God who gives the growth. He who plants and he who *waters* are equal, and each shall receive (*lēmpsetai*; from the verb *lambanein*) his wages according to his labor. For we are God's fellow workers; you are God's field (*geōrgion*), God's building. (1 Cor 3:5-9)

> For land which has drunk the *rain* that often falls upon it, and brings forth vegetation useful to those for whose sake it is cultivated (*geōrgeitai*), receives (*metalambanei*; from the root *lambanein*) a blessing from God. But if it bears thorns and thistles,

---

[4] See my comments in *Gal* 27-31.

it is worthless and near to being cursed; its end is to be burned. (Heb 6:7-8)

He exhorts the believers not to be *nōthroi* (sluggish, 6:12a; dull, 5:11), but to be "imitators of those who through faith and patience inherit the promises" (6:12b). The reason behind such urging follows the same logic found in 2 Corinthians 1.[5] Although Paul is "sure" (confident, *pepeismetha*) of their ultimate salvation (Heb 6:9), nevertheless, the believers are to persevere "until the end" (v.11) in the work of love, which is eminently expressed through the *diakonia*, the service of table fellowship (v.10), especially toward the less fortunate. This teaching pervades the Pauline corpus:

> For through the Spirit, by faith, we wait for the hope of righteousness. For in Christ Jesus neither circumcision nor uncircumcision is of any avail, but faith working through love. (Gal 5:5-6)

> I thank my God in all my remembrance of you, always in every prayer of mine for you all making my prayer with joy, thankful for your partnership in the gospel from the first day until now. And I am sure that he who began a good work in you will bring it to completion at the day of Jesus Christ. It is right for me to feel thus about you all, because I hold you in my heart, for you are all partakers with me of grace, both in my imprisonment and in the defense and confirmation of the gospel. For God is my witness, how I yearn for you all with the affection of Christ Jesus. And it is my prayer that your love may abound more and more, with knowledge and all discernment, so that you may approve what is excellent, and may be pure and blameless for the day of Christ, filled with the fruits of righteousness which come through Jesus Christ, to the glory and praise of God. (Phil 1:3-11)

---

[5] See my comments in *C-2Cor* 28-29; 53-56.

For this reason, because I have heard of your faith in the Lord Jesus and your love toward all the saints, I do not cease to give thanks for you, remembering you in my prayers, that the God of our Lord Jesus Christ, the Father of glory, may give you a spirit of wisdom and of revelation in the knowledge of him, having the eyes of your hearts enlightened, that you may know what is the hope to which he has called you, what are the riches of his glorious inheritance in the saints. (Eph 1:15-18)

We always thank God, the Father of our Lord Jesus Christ, when we pray for you, because we have heard of your faith in Christ Jesus and of the love which you have for all the saints, because of the hope laid up for you in heaven. (Col 1:3-5)

We give thanks to God always for you all, constantly mentioning you in our prayers, remembering before our God and Father your work of faith and labor of love and steadfastness of hope in our Lord Jesus Christ. (1Thess 1:2-3)

We are bound to give thanks to God always for you, brethren, as is fitting, because your faith is growing abundantly, and the love of every one of you for one another is increasing. (2 Thess 1:3)

Vv. 13-20 ¹³Τῷ γὰρ Ἀβραὰμ ἐπαγγειλάμενος ὁ θεός, ἐπεὶ κατ' οὐδενὸς εἶχεν μείζονος ὀμόσαι, ὤμοσεν καθ' ἑαυτοῦ ¹⁴λέγων· εἰ μὴν εὐλογῶν εὐλογήσω σε καὶ πληθύνων πληθυνῶ σε· ¹⁵καὶ οὕτως μακροθυμήσας ἐπέτυχεν τῆς ἐπαγγελίας. ¹⁶ἄνθρωποι γὰρ κατὰ τοῦ μείζονος ὀμνύουσιν, καὶ πάσης αὐτοῖς ἀντιλογίας πέρας εἰς βεβαίωσιν ὁ ὅρκος· ¹⁷ἐν ᾧ περισσότερον βουλόμενος ὁ θεὸς ἐπιδεῖξαι τοῖς κληρονόμοις τῆς ἐπαγγελίας τὸ ἀμετάθετον τῆς βουλῆς αὐτοῦ ἐμεσίτευσεν ὅρκῳ, ¹⁸ἵνα διὰ δύο πραγμάτων ἀμεταθέτων, ἐν οἷς ἀδύνατον ψεύσασθαι [τὸν] θεόν, ἰσχυρὰν παράκλησιν ἔχωμεν οἱ καταφυγόντες κρατῆσαι τῆς προκειμένης ἐλπίδος· ¹⁹ἣν ὡς ἄγκυραν ἔχομεν τῆς ψυχῆς ἀσφαλῆ τε καὶ βεβαίαν καὶ εἰσερχομένην εἰς τὸ ἐσώτερον τοῦ καταπετάσματος, ²⁰ὅπου πρόδρομος ὑπὲρ ἡμῶν εἰσῆλθεν Ἰησοῦς, κατὰ τὴν τάξιν Μελχισέδεκ ἀρχιερεὺς γενόμενος εἰς τὸν αἰῶνα.

¹³For when God made a promise to Abraham, since he had no one greater by whom to swear, he swore by himself, ¹⁴saying, "Surely I will bless you and multiply you." ¹⁵And thus Abraham, having patiently endured, obtained the promise. ¹⁶Men indeed swear by a greater than themselves, and in all their disputes an oath is final for confirmation. ¹⁷So when God desired to show more convincingly to the heirs of the promise the unchangeable character of his purpose, he interposed with an oath, ¹⁸so that through two unchangeable things, in which it is impossible that God should prove false, we who have fled for refuge might have strong encouragement to seize the hope set before us. ¹⁹We have this as a sure and steadfast anchor of the soul, a hope that enters into the inner shrine behind the curtain, ²⁰where Jesus has gone as a forerunner on our behalf, having become a high priest for ever after the order of Melchizedek.

Verses 13-20 function as a hinge between what preceded and what will follow. Abraham is used as an example for the addressees to emulate in their "faith and patience (*makrothymias*)" (Heb 6:12). Although the divine promise of blessing (v.14) was as "sure" as can be, having been given with the most solemn oath possible (vv.13 and 16), Abraham still had to "patiently endure" (*makrothymēsas*) in order to behold the fulfillment of that promise (v.15), that is, God's gift of Isaac (Gen 22:1-19). Hence, "we" (Heb 6:18), "the heirs of the promise" (v.17), are to follow suit, and one day "seize the hope set before us" (v.18). This hope is "a sure and steadfast anchor" (v.19), not only because of "the unchangeable character of God's purpose" (v.17), but also because his promise was fully realized in Jesus, who preceded us—we who are his "house" (3:1-6)—into the heavenly Jerusalem (6:19) as a "forerunner on our behalf" (v.20a), just as the "high priest enters into the inner shrine behind the curtain" on behalf of the people. By quoting

Psalm 110:4 (Heb 6:20), the author has prepared for his discussion of the relationship between Abraham and Melchizedek in chapter 7.

Chapter 7

Vv. 7:1-28 ¹Οὗτος γὰρ ὁ Μελχισέδεκ, βασιλεὺς Σαλήμ, ἱερεὺς τοῦ θεοῦ τοῦ ὑψίστου, ὁ συναντήσας Ἀβραὰμ ὑποστρέφοντι ἀπὸ τῆς κοπῆς τῶν βασιλέων καὶ εὐλογήσας αὐτόν, ²ᾧ καὶ δεκάτην ἀπὸ πάντων ἐμέρισεν Ἀβραάμ, πρῶτον μὲν ἑρμηνευόμενος βασιλεὺς δικαιοσύνης ἔπειτα δὲ καὶ βασιλεὺς Σαλήμ, ὅ ἐστιν βασιλεὺς εἰρήνης, ³ἀπάτωρ ἀμήτωρ ἀγενεαλόγητος, μήτε ἀρχὴν ἡμερῶν μήτε ζωῆς τέλος ἔχων, ἀφωμοιωμένος δὲ τῷ υἱῷ τοῦ θεοῦ, μένει ἱερεὺς εἰς τὸ διηνεκές. ⁴Θεωρεῖτε δὲ πηλίκος οὗτος, ᾧ [καὶ] δεκάτην Ἀβραὰμ ἔδωκεν ἐκ τῶν ἀκροθινίων ὁ πατριάρχης. ⁵καὶ οἱ μὲν ἐκ τῶν υἱῶν Λευὶ τὴν ἱερατείαν λαμβάνοντες ἐντολὴν ἔχουσιν ἀποδεκατοῦν τὸν λαὸν κατὰ τὸν νόμον, τοῦτ' ἔστιν τοὺς ἀδελφοὺς αὐτῶν, καίπερ ἐξεληλυθότας ἐκ τῆς ὀσφύος Ἀβραάμ· ⁶ὁ δὲ μὴ γενεαλογούμενος ἐξ αὐτῶν δεδεκάτωκεν Ἀβραὰμ καὶ τὸν ἔχοντα τὰς ἐπαγγελίας εὐλόγηκεν. ⁷χωρὶς δὲ πάσης ἀντιλογίας τὸ ἔλαττον ὑπὸ τοῦ κρείττονος εὐλογεῖται. ⁸καὶ ὧδε μὲν δεκάτας ἀποθνῄσκοντες ἄνθρωποι λαμβάνουσιν, ἐκεῖ δὲ μαρτυρούμενος ὅτι ζῇ. ⁹καὶ ὡς ἔπος εἰπεῖν, δι' Ἀβραὰμ καὶ Λευὶ ὁ δεκάτας λαμβάνων δεδεκάτωται· ¹⁰ἔτι γὰρ ἐν τῇ ὀσφύϊ τοῦ πατρὸς ἦν ὅτε συνήντησεν αὐτῷ Μελχισέδεκ. ¹¹Εἰ μὲν οὖν τελείωσις διὰ τῆς Λευιτικῆς ἱερωσύνης ἦν, ὁ λαὸς γὰρ ἐπ' αὐτῆς νενομοθέτηται, τίς ἔτι χρεία κατὰ τὴν τάξιν Μελχισέδεκ ἕτερον ἀνίστασθαι ἱερέα καὶ οὐ κατὰ τὴν τάξιν Ἀαρὼν λέγεσθαι; ¹²μετατιθεμένης γὰρ τῆς ἱερωσύνης ἐξ ἀνάγκης καὶ νόμου μετάθεσις γίνεται. ¹³ἐφ' ὃν γὰρ λέγεται ταῦτα, φυλῆς ἑτέρας μετέσχηκεν, ἀφ' ἧς οὐδεὶς προσέσχηκεν τῷ θυσιαστηρίῳ· ¹⁴πρόδηλον γὰρ ὅτι ἐξ Ἰούδα ἀνατέταλκεν ὁ κύριος ἡμῶν, εἰς ἣν φυλὴν περὶ ἱερέων οὐδὲν Μωϋσῆς ἐλάλησεν. ¹⁵καὶ περισσότερον ἔτι κατάδηλόν ἐστιν, εἰ κατὰ τὴν ὁμοιότητα Μελχισέδεκ ἀνίσταται ἱερεὺς ἕτερος, ¹⁶ὃς οὐ κατὰ νόμον ἐντολῆς σαρκίνης γέγονεν ἀλλὰ κατὰ δύναμιν ζωῆς ἀκαταλύτου. ¹⁷μαρτυρεῖται γὰρ ὅτι σὺ ἱερεὺς εἰς τὸν αἰῶνα κατὰ τὴν τάξιν Μελχισέδεκ. ¹⁸ἀθέτησις μὲν γὰρ γίνεται προαγούσης ἐντολῆς διὰ τὸ αὐτῆς ἀσθενὲς καὶ ἀνωφελές- ¹⁹οὐδὲν γὰρ ἐτελείωσεν ὁ νόμος- ἐπεισαγωγὴ δὲ κρείττονος ἐλπίδος δι' ἧς ἐγγίζομεν τῷ θεῷ. ²⁰Καὶ καθ' ὅσον οὐ χωρὶς ὀρκωμοσίας· οἱ μὲν γὰρ χωρὶς ὀρκωμοσίας εἰσὶν ἱερεῖς γεγονότες, ²¹ὁ δὲ μετὰ ὀρκωμοσίας διὰ τοῦ λέγοντος πρὸς αὐτόν· ὤμοσεν κύριος καὶ οὐ μεταμεληθήσεται· σὺ ἱερεὺς εἰς τὸν αἰῶνα. ²²κατὰ τοσοῦτο [καὶ] κρείττονος διαθήκης γέγονεν ἔγγυος Ἰησοῦς. ²³Καὶ οἱ μὲν πλείονές εἰσιν γεγονότες ἱερεῖς διὰ τὸ θανάτῳ κωλύεσθαι παραμένειν· ²⁴ὁ δὲ διὰ τὸ μένειν αὐτὸν εἰς τὸν αἰῶνα ἀπαράβατον ἔχει τὴν ἱερωσύνην· ²⁵ὅθεν καὶ σῴζειν εἰς τὸ παντελὲς δύναται τοὺς προσερχομένους δι' αὐτοῦ τῷ θεῷ, πάντοτε ζῶν εἰς τὸ ἐντυγχάνειν ὑπὲρ αὐτῶν. ²⁶Τοιοῦτος γὰρ ἡμῖν καὶ ἔπρεπεν ἀρχιερεύς, ὅσιος ἄκακος ἀμίαντος, κεχωρισμένος ἀπὸ τῶν ἁμαρτωλῶν καὶ ὑψηλότερος τῶν οὐρανῶν γενόμενος, ²⁷ὃς οὐκ ἔχει καθ' ἡμέραν ἀνάγκην, ὥσπερ οἱ ἀρχιερεῖς, πρότερον ὑπὲρ τῶν ἰδίων ἁμαρτιῶν θυσίας ἀναφέρειν ἔπειτα τῶν τοῦ λαοῦ· τοῦτο γὰρ ἐποίησεν ἐφάπαξ ἑαυτὸν ἀνενέγκας. ²⁸ὁ νόμος γὰρ ἀνθρώπους καθίστησιν ἀρχιερεῖς ἔχοντας ἀσθένειαν, ὁ λόγος δὲ τῆς ὀρκωμοσίας τῆς μετὰ τὸν νόμον υἱὸν εἰς τὸν αἰῶνα τετελειωμένον.

¹For this Melchizedek, king of Salem, priest of the Most High God, met Abraham returning from the slaughter of the kings and blessed him; ²and to him Abraham apportioned a tenth part of everything. He is first, by translation of his name, king of righteousness, and then he is also king of Salem, that is, king of peace. ³He is without father or mother or genealogy, and has neither beginning of days nor end of life, but resembling the Son of God he continues a priest for ever. ⁴See how great he is! Abraham the patriarch gave him a tithe of the spoils. ⁵And those descendants of Levi who receive the priestly office have a commandment in the law to take tithes from the people, that is, from their brethren, though these also are descended from Abraham. ⁶But this man who has not their genealogy received tithes from Abraham and blessed him who had the promises. ⁷It is beyond dispute that the inferior is blessed by the superior. ⁸Here tithes are received by mortal men; there, by one of whom it is testified that he lives. ⁹One might even say that Levi himself, who receives tithes, paid tithes through Abraham, ¹⁰for he was still in the loins of his ancestor when Melchizedek met him. ⁱ¹Now if perfection had been attainable through the Levitical priesthood (for under it the people received the law), what further need would there have been for another priest to arise after the order of Melchizedek, rather than one named after the order of Aaron? ¹²For when there is a change in the priesthood, there is necessarily a change in the law as well. ¹³For the one of whom these things are spoken belonged to another tribe, from which no one has ever served at the altar. ¹⁴For it is evident that our Lord was descended from Judah, and in connection with that tribe Moses said nothing about priests. ¹⁵This becomes even more evident when another priest arises in the likeness of Melchizedek, ¹⁶who has become a priest, not according to a legal requirement concerning bodily descent but by the power of an indestructible life. ¹⁷For it is witnessed of him, "Thou art a priest for ever, after the order of Melchizedek." ¹⁸On the one hand, a former commandment is set aside because of its weakness and uselessness ¹⁹(for the law made nothing perfect); on the other hand, a better hope is introduced, through which we draw near to God. ²⁰And it was not without an oath. ²¹Those who formerly became priests took their office without an oath, but this one was addressed with an oath, "The Lord has sworn and will not change his mind, 'Thou art a priest for ever.'" ²²This makes Jesus the surety of a better covenant. ²³The former priests were many in number, because they were prevented by death from continuing in office; ²⁴but he holds his priesthood permanently, because he continues for ever. ²⁵Consequently he is able for all time to save those who draw near to God through him, since he always lives to make intercession for them. ²⁶For it was fitting that we should have such a high priest, holy, blameless, unstained, separated from sinners, exalted above the heavens. ²⁷He has no need, like those high priests, to offer sacrifices daily, first for his own sins and then for those of the people; he did this once for all when he *offered up himself.* ²⁸*Indeed, the law appoints men in their weakness as high priests, but the word of the oath, which came later than the law, appoints a Son who has been made perfect for ever.*

The author's choice of Abraham as the prime example of the effort necessary to persevere on the way of righteousness, in spite of the full assuredness of the divine promise, is warranted. The reason is given in scripture itself:

> The Lord said, "Shall I hide from Abraham what I am about to do, seeing that Abraham shall become a great and mighty nation, and all the nations of the earth shall bless themselves by him? No, for I have chosen him, that he may charge his children and his household after him to keep the way of the Lord by doing righteousness and justice; so that the Lord may bring to Abraham what he has promised him." (Gen 18:17-19)

> Now there was a famine in the land, besides the former famine that was in the days of Abraham. And Isaac went to Gerar, to Abimelech king of the Philistines. And the Lord appeared to him, and said, "Do not go down to Egypt; dwell in the land of which I shall tell you. Sojourn in this land, and I will be with you, and will bless you; for to you and to your descendants I will give all these lands, and I will fulfil the oath which I swore to Abraham your father. I will multiply your descendants as the stars of heaven, and will give to your descendants all these lands; and by your descendants all the nations of the earth shall bless themselves: because Abraham obeyed my voice and kept my charge, my commandments, my statutes, and my laws." (26:1-5)

Still, and more importantly for the overall argument, it is the relationship between Abraham and Melchizedek that is paramount for two reasons. First, the encounter between them is reported very early in Abraham's life, shortly after he had received the divine blessing (12:1-3). Moreover, that blessing is iterated again during that encounter:

> And Melchizedek king of Salem brought out bread and wine; he was priest of God Most High. And he blessed him and said, "Blessed be Abram by God Most High, maker of heaven and earth; and blessed be God Most High, who has delivered your enemies into your hand!" And Abram gave him a tenth of everything. (Gen 14:18-20)

Secondly, the only instances in the Old Testament where one hears of Melchizedek are in Genesis 14 and Psalm 110. Listening closely to these passages, one will readily notice the full correspondence in both cases. Melchizedek is expressly introduced as both king and priest, but it is his function as priest that is underscored: "He [Melchizedek] was priest of God Most High … And Abram gave him a tenth of everything";[1] "Thou art a priest for ever, after the order of Melchizedek."[2] So the author's use of Genesis 14 in his argument in Hebrews is totally justified.

However, pointing out the meaning of the original Hebrew twice in one verse (Heb 7:2) is unique in the New Testament: "For this Melchizedek, king of Salem, priest of the Most High God, met Abraham returning from the slaughter of the kings and blessed him; and to him Abraham apportioned a tenth part of everything. He is *first* (Greek *prōton*), by translation of his name, king of righteousness, and *then* [*after that*, KJV] (Greek *epeita*) he is also king of Salem, that is, king of peace (*eirēnēs*)." (vv.1-2) Notice that the author introduces a temporal sequence (first … then [after that]) in his explanatory comment, which is not in Genesis; there both the name Melchizedek and the title

---

[1] Gen 14:18, 20.
[2] Ps 110:4.

"king of Salem" are appositional. The temporal sequence is used again in Hebrews 7:26-27: "For it was fitting that we should have such a high priest, holy, blameless, unstained, separated from sinners, exalted above the heavens. He has no need, like those high priests, to offer sacrifices daily, *first* (Greek *proteron*) for his own sins and *then* (Greek *epeita*) for those of the people; he did this once for all when he offered up himself." What makes the case for an express intentionality on the author's part in this regard is that while the reference to righteousness is warranted due to its centrality in the overall argument (1:9;[3] 5:13), "peace" is not addressed until the end of the letter (12:14; 13:20). To explain its use here (7:2), one must consider "peace" as a translation of a city name. In the Book of Psalms, from which the central reference to Melchizedek is taken (110:4), one will readily notice the reference to Salem as a city name: "In Judah God is known, his name is great in Israel. His abode has been established in Salem, his dwelling place in Zion." (Ps 76:1-2) The Septuagint actually "translates" Salem into its meaning in these verses: "God is known in Judea: his name is great in Israel. And his place has been *in peace* (*en eirēnē*), and his dwelling-place in Sion." (LXX Ps 75:2-3) Zion, God's city, is depicted, at the end of the Book of Psalms, as the city of peace established by the Lord himself:

> Praise the Lord! For it is good to sing praises to our God; for he is gracious, and a song of praise is seemly. The Lord builds up Jerusalem; he gathers the outcasts of Israel ... Praise the Lord, O Jerusalem! Praise your God, O Zion! For he strengthens the bars of your gates; he blesses your sons within you. He makes peace (Greek *eirēnēn*) in your borders; he fills you with the finest of the wheat. (Ps 147:1-2, 12-14)

---

[3] The original Greek for RSV "righteous" (scepter) in v.8 is *tēs evthytētos* ([scepter] of uprightness).

And this is what one hears at the end of Hebrews:

> Therefore lift your drooping hands and strengthen your weak knees, and make straight paths for your feet, so that what is lame may not be put out of joint but rather be healed. Strive for peace (*eirēnēn*) *with all men*, and for the holiness without which no one will see the Lord ... For you have not come to what may be touched, a blazing fire, and darkness, and gloom, and a tempest, and the sound of a trumpet, and a voice whose words made the hearers entreat that no further messages be spoken to them. For they could not endure the order that was given, "If even a beast touches the mountain, it shall be stoned." Indeed, so terrifying was the sight that Moses said, "I tremble with fear." But you have come to Mount Zion and to the city of the living God, the heavenly Jerusalem, and to innumerable angels in festal gathering ... Now may the God of peace (*eirēnēs*) who brought again from the dead our Lord Jesus, the great shepherd of the sheep, by the blood of the eternal covenant, equip you with everything good that you may do his will, working in you that which is pleasing in his sight, through Jesus Christ; to whom be glory for ever and ever. Amen. (12:12-14, 18-22; 13:20-21)

By underscoring the element of peace as the consequence of righteousness in 7:2, the author is preparing for the conclusion of his argument. He is bidding his addressees to follow the path of righteousness so that they may enjoy the peace of God that ultimately will be implemented through God's son, "the high priest after the order of Melchizedek (king of righteousness)," the "king of Salem (peace)."[4]

Unfortunately, in classical theology Hebrews 7:3 is understood as referring to an eternal being that was incarnate in time. This, however, is not the case. First of all, the verse, "He is without

---

[4] Gen 14:18.

father or mother or genealogy, and has neither beginning of days nor end of life, but resembling the Son of God he continues a priest for ever," is describing Melchizedek not Christ. "Theologically speaking," to conclude that Melchizedek is an eternal being appearing as a human is a proposition no one is willing to uphold. It would not make sense if there were a person besides and *before* Christ who had the same "theological" value ascribed to Christ! Furthermore, it is Melchizedek who is likened to the Son of God, not vice versa. More importantly, when the text of Hebrews speaks of the "Son of God," it does so in a very specific way. From the beginning of the letter, he is presented along the lines of Psalms 2:7 and 110:4, namely, as a monarch assigned by the deity at the day of enthronement. On that day of enthronement he is "begotten" by the deity. Put otherwise, one is not king until one "becomes" king. A king does not need to be enthroned! One is enthroned *as* king by the deity in order to become king in the eyes of the people. One becomes monarch on the "today" of one's enthronement (Ps 2:7) when one is seated by the deity at its right hand (110:1). Such took place at the end of Jesus' life (Phil 2:8-11; Mk 16:19; Acts 2:31-33; 5:30-31), not in a presumed "eternity." It is at the actual point in time when one accedes to the divine throne (Ps 45:6) that one starts looking divine and thus "eternal." In this sense and at that point in time, the monarch as "Son of God" is *co-eternal* with the deity. The deity is *eternal* per se and never *co-eternal* with the monarch.[5] Only teenagers are confident that their parents look like them, not they like their parents! So what the author of Hebrews is maintaining is that Melchizedek appears *in scripture*

---

[5] Notice how even the Nicene Creed is adamant to present the Lord Jesus Christ as "Light *from* Light" and "God *from* God," given that the *one God* is specifically the Father Almighty.

as "resembling" the Christ presented *in the same scripture*. In which sense?

Having "neither beginning of days nor end of life" is tantamount to being "eternal." The issue that remains to be explained is "without father or mother or genealogy" (Heb 7:3) and to explain this without using the classical theology's statement "without father according to his humanity and without mother according to his godhead." In the original statement of 7:3, *apatōr, amētōr, agenealogētos* is an appositional series of adjectives whose literal translation is "fatherless, motherless, a-genealogical." It is an extensive metaphor that boils down to being "without ascending genealogy or progeny," that is to say, "without a human (fleshly) lineage," "without a family tree." The only scriptural person that fits this description is the new David, the promised eschatological messiah who stands on his own as monarch "forever," and thus is in no need of progeny. This is in contrast to the earlier David, son of Jesse, who established the Davidic dynasty: "For thus says the Lord: David shall never lack a man to sit on the throne of the house of Israel" (Jer 33:17); "Instead of your fathers shall be your sons; you will make them princes in all the earth" (Ps 45:16). The new David will be enthroned in the new Zion, a city "built in heaven" (Heb 12:22; see also Gal 4:26; Phil 3:20; Rev 21:2) and thus has no human "history."

By the same token, the new David stands on his own as the "once and for all upcoming ages" designee Son of God, without predecessors or successors. Such is a scriptural reality, that is, a reality that exists solely within the confines and parameters of the scriptural text, as evidenced in the ending of the Book of Revelation:

> I warn (*martyrō*; witness to, confess openly to) every one who hears the words of the prophecy of this book (writ): if any one adds to them, God will add to him the plagues described (*gegrammena*; written, scripturalized) in this book (writ), and if any one takes away from the words of the book (writ) of this prophecy, God will take away his share in the tree of life and in the holy city, which are described (*gegrammena*; written, scripturalized) in this book (writ). (22:18-19)

In this same sense, when one "hears" of Melchizedek in Genesis 14, one encounters aurally, acoustically, someone who suddenly appears and then suddenly vanishes, without any "history" save that he is the king of Salem and priest of the most High God, just as he is described in Psalm 110. In other words, scripturally, Melchizedek is a prototype of the new David, the king and high priest of the upcoming "city of peace." The connection between the two is all the more compelling when one considers that in Jeremiah both the new David and the city of God are depicted in terms of righteousness, which is subsumed in the name Melchizedek, "king of righteousness" (Heb 7:2):

> Behold, the days are coming, says the Lord, when I will raise up for David a righteous Branch, and he shall reign as king and deal wisely, and shall execute justice and righteousness in the land. In his days Judah will be saved, and Israel will dwell securely. And this is the name by which he will be called: "The Lord is our righteousness." (Jer 23:5-6)

> Thus says the Lord of hosts, the God of Israel: "Once more they shall use these words in the land of Judah and in its cities, when I restore their fortunes: 'The Lord bless you, O habitation of righteousness, O holy hill!'" (31:23)

> Behold, the days are coming, says the Lord, when I will fulfil the promise I made to the house of Israel and the house of Judah. In

those days and at that time I will cause a righteous Branch to spring forth for David; and he shall execute justice and righteousness in the land. In those days Judah will be saved and Jerusalem will dwell securely. And this is the name by which it will be called: "The Lord is our righteousness." (33:14-16)

The author's main interest is to show that the temple, together with its services, is obsolete. To do this, he zeroes in on the issue of the tithes Abraham paid to Melchizedek. In the Law, tithing is for the Levitical priests. Since Levi, the ancestor of the priesthood, was "in the loins" of Abraham when Abraham paid tithes to Melchizedek, it as though the Levitical priests paid tithes to the "king of righteousness," the prototype of the coming new David who, in scripture, is from the tribe of Judah whence came the first David (Gen 49:8-10; Rom 1:3; Rev 5:5). This explains why, in the Gospels, "Son of David" is tantamount to messiah.[6] More importantly, however, is that Jesus' priesthood is not commissioned through genealogical progeny, but by the power of God (Heb 7:16-17; Ps 110:2), as is his kingship (Rom 1:4; Ps 2:7) at his being raised from the dead to be seated at the divine right hand:

> This becomes even more evident when another priest arises in the likeness of Melchizedek, who has become a priest, not according to a legal requirement concerning bodily descent but by the power of an indestructible life. For it is witnessed of him, "Thou art a priest for ever, after the order of Melchizedek." (Heb 7:15-17)

> Paul, a servant of Jesus Christ, called to be an apostle, set apart for the gospel of God which he promised beforehand through his prophets in the holy scriptures, the gospel concerning his Son, who was descended from David according to the flesh and

---

[6] Mt 1:1; 9:27; 12:23; 15:22; 20:30-31//Mk 10:47-48//Lk 18:38-39; Mt 21:9, 15; 22:41-44//Mk 12:35.

designated Son of God in power according to the Spirit of holiness by his resurrection from the dead, Jesus Christ our Lord. (Rom 1:1-4)

In comparison with the "once and for all" priesthood of Christ (Heb 7:24-25, 28), the mortal Levitical priesthood is perpetrated through an incessant genealogy (v.23). Unlike Levitical priests who offer sacrifices for their own sins (7:27), Christ, being sinless (v.26; see also 4:15), has no need to do so. In order to underscore the importance of God's decision regarding this matter, the author describes it as an oath in order to emphasize that God's decision stands for good and ever (7:20-21) and that he would not change his mind (Psalm 110:4). This is what guarantees the assuredness of a better hope (Heb 7:19; see also 3:6; 6:11, 18-19) and a better covenant (7:22), the better covenant being the Jeremianic new covenant which will be referred to shortly (Heb 8:8-12; Jer 31:31-34).

The author ends chapter 7 by using the same approach he used earlier in chapters 3-4: in spite of the fact that "the law is holy, and the commandment is holy and just and good" (Rom 7:12), the people continually disobeyed the Law. God, in his mercy, offered their progeny another chance to implement his will. In the past, a new set of priests as well as new sacrifices for the sins of the people were needed to atone for the people's repeated transgressions. Thus the divine law appeared de facto to be "weak and useless": "On the one hand, a former commandment is set aside because of its weakness and uselessness (for the law made nothing perfect)." (Heb 7:18-19a) In the same scripture we hear that "on the other hand, a better hope is introduced, through which we draw near to God" (v.19b). Moreover, the assuredness of such hope lies in that it was uttered through a word that came *later* than the Law: "Indeed, the law appoints men in their weakness[7] as high priests, but the word of the oath, which came later than the law, appoints a Son who has been made perfect for ever." (v.28)

The aspect of "lateness" is an essential factor in the author's entire argument. In the Old Testament scripture the order is the following: first the Law (*torah*; Pentateuch), then the Prophets (*nebi'im*) among which are the Books of Joshua and Jeremiah, and finally the Writings (*ketubim*) wherein is the Book of Psalms. Earlier, in Hebrews 3 and 4, the quotation from Psalm 95:7-11 (Heb 3:7a-11) reflected the new offer of restoration after the failure under Moses (Heb 3:8 [Ps 95:8]) and Joshua (Heb 4:8). The sequence in Hebrews is: Law, Jeremiah, Psalms. The author is nimbly preparing for the lengthy quotation from Jeremiah 31:31-34 in Hebrews 8:8-12 concerning the "new covenant" through the reference to the "new covenant" in Hebrews 7:22 in parallel with the "better hope" (v.19b).

---

[7] Corresponding to the "weakness" mentioned in v.18.

Chapter 8

Vv. 8:1-13 *¹Κεφάλαιον δὲ ἐπὶ τοῖς λεγομένοις, τοιοῦτον ἔχομεν ἀρχιερέα, ὃς ἐκάθισεν ἐν δεξιᾷ τοῦ θρόνου τῆς μεγαλωσύνης ἐν τοῖς οὐρανοῖς, ² τῶν ἁγίων λειτουργὸς καὶ τῆς σκηνῆς τῆς ἀληθινῆς, ἣν ἔπηξεν ὁ κύριος, οὐκ ἄνθρωπος. ³Πᾶς γὰρ ἀρχιερεὺς εἰς τὸ προσφέρειν δῶρά τε καὶ θυσίας καθίσταται· ὅθεν ἀναγκαῖον ἔχειν τι καὶ τοῦτον ὃ προσενέγκῃ. ⁴εἰ μὲν οὖν ἦν ἐπὶ γῆς, οὐδ᾽ ἂν ἦν ἱερεύς, ὄντων τῶν προσφερόντων κατὰ νόμον τὰ δῶρα· ⁵οἵτινες ὑποδείγματι καὶ σκιᾷ λατρεύουσιν τῶν ἐπουρανίων, καθὼς κεχρημάτισται Μωϋσῆς μέλλων ἐπιτελεῖν τὴν σκηνήν· ὅρα γάρ φησιν, ποιήσεις πάντα κατὰ τὸν τύπον τὸν δειχθέντα σοι ἐν τῷ ὄρει· ⁶νυν[ὶ] δὲ διαφορωτέρας τέτυχεν λειτουργίας, ὅσῳ καὶ κρείττονός ἐστιν διαθήκης μεσίτης, ἥτις ἐπὶ κρείττοσιν ἐπαγγελίαις νενομοθέτηται. ⁷Εἰ γὰρ ἡ πρώτη ἐκείνη ἦν ἄμεμπτος, οὐκ ἂν δευτέρας ἐζητεῖτο τόπος. ⁸μεμφόμενος γὰρ αὐτοὺς λέγει· ἰδοὺ ἡμέραι ἔρχονται, λέγει κύριος, καὶ συντελέσω ἐπὶ τὸν οἶκον Ἰσραὴλ καὶ ἐπὶ τὸν οἶκον Ἰούδα διαθήκην καινήν, ⁹οὐ κατὰ τὴν διαθήκην, ἣν ἐποίησα τοῖς πατράσιν αὐτῶν ἐν ἡμέρᾳ ἐπιλαβομένου μου τῆς χειρὸς αὐτῶν ἐξαγαγεῖν αὐτοὺς ἐκ γῆς Αἰγύπτου, ὅτι αὐτοὶ οὐκ ἐνέμειναν ἐν τῇ διαθήκῃ μου, κἀγὼ ἠμέλησα αὐτῶν, λέγει κύριος· ¹⁰ὅτι αὕτη ἡ διαθήκη, ἣν διαθήσομαι τῷ οἴκῳ Ἰσραὴλ μετὰ τὰς ἡμέρας ἐκείνας, λέγει κύριος· διδοὺς νόμους μου εἰς τὴν διάνοιαν αὐτῶν καὶ ἐπὶ καρδίας αὐτῶν ἐπιγράψω αὐτούς, καὶ ἔσομαι αὐτοῖς εἰς θεόν, καὶ αὐτοὶ ἔσονταί μοι εἰς λαόν· ¹¹καὶ οὐ μὴ διδάξωσιν ἕκαστος τὸν πολίτην αὐτοῦ καὶ ἕκαστος τὸν ἀδελφὸν αὐτοῦ λέγων· γνῶθι τὸν κύριον, ὅτι πάντες εἰδήσουσίν με ἀπὸ μικροῦ ἕως μεγάλου αὐτῶν, ¹²ὅτι ἵλεως ἔσομαι ταῖς ἀδικίαις αὐτῶν καὶ τῶν ἁμαρτιῶν αὐτῶν οὐ μὴ μνησθῶ ἔτι. ¹³ἐν τῷ λέγειν καινὴν πεπαλαίωκεν τὴν πρώτην· τὸ δὲ παλαιούμενον καὶ γηράσκον ἐγγὺς ἀφανισμοῦ.*

¹Now the point in what we are saying is this: we have such a high priest, one who is seated at the right hand of the throne of the Majesty in heaven, ²a minister in the sanctuary and the true tent which is set up not by man but by the Lord. ³For every high priest is appointed to offer gifts and sacrifices; hence it is necessary for this priest also to have something to offer. ⁴Now if he were on earth, he would not be a priest at all, since there are priests who offer gifts according to the law. ⁵They serve a copy and shadow of the heavenly sanctuary; for when Moses was about to erect the tent, he was instructed by God, saying, "See that you make everything according to the pattern which was shown you on the mountain." ⁶But as it is, Christ has obtained a ministry which is as much more excellent than the old as the covenant he mediates is better, since it is enacted on better promises. ⁷For if that first covenant had been faultless, there would have been no occasion for a second. ⁸For he finds fault with them when he says: "The days will come, says the Lord, when I will establish a new covenant with the house of Israel and with the house of Judah; ⁹not like the covenant that I made with their fathers on the day when I took them by the hand to lead them out of the land of Egypt; for they did not continue in my covenant, and so I paid no heed to them, says the Lord. ¹⁰This is the covenant that I will make with the house of Israel after those days, says the Lord: I will put my laws into their minds, and write them on their hearts, and I will be their God, and they shall be my people. ¹¹And they shall not teach every one his fellow or every one his brother, saying, 'Know the Lord,' for all shall know me, from the least of them to the greatest. ¹²For I will be merciful toward their iniquities, and I will remember their sins no more." ¹³In speaking of a new covenant he treats the first as obsolete. And what is becoming obsolete and growing old is ready to vanish away.

In chapter 8 the author recapitulates[1] (8:1a) all he had said earlier. The main point of his argument is that what made the first covenant faulty was the disobedience of the people: "For if

---

[1] This is the meaning of the original *kephalaion*.

that first covenant had been *faultless*, there would have been no occasion for a second, for *he finds fault with them*" (8:8). In continuation of this verse, God utters the promise of a new covenant (vv.8-12). The new covenant, however, is still bound to the *same* Law as that of the now obsolete covenant: "But as it is, Christ has obtained a ministry which is as much more excellent than the old as the covenant he mediates is better, since it is enacted (*nenomothetētai* [from the root *nomos*, law]; it is "legalized," it is *set as a law*) on better promises." (v.6) The author is not reinventing the wheel, but merely introducing the passage on the new covenant from Jeremiah:

> The days will come, says the Lord, when I will establish a new covenant with the house of Israel and with the house of Judah; not like the covenant that I made with their fathers on the day when I took them by the hand to lead them out of the land of Egypt; for they did not continue in my covenant, and so I paid no heed to them, says the Lord. This is the covenant that I will make with the house of Israel after those days, says the Lord: I will put my *laws* (*nomous*) into their minds, and write them on their hearts, and I will be their God, and they shall be my people. And they shall not teach every one his fellow or every one his brother, saying, "Know the Lord," for all shall know me, from the least of them to the greatest. For I will be merciful toward their iniquities, and I will remember their sins no more. (Heb 8:8a-12; Jer LXX 38:31-34 [MT 31:31-34]).

By using the plural "laws" of the LXX text instead of the original Hebrew singular "law" (*torah*),[2] the author is indirectly underscoring that the new covenant contains the entire set of laws of the first, that is, the Mosaic covenant. The novelty lies

---

[2] See also the other instance in 2 Kg 14:6: "according to what is written in the book of the law of Moses" (Hebrew); "according to what is written in the book of the laws of Moses" (Greek).

solely in the location of the writ: on the hearts of the people instead of on stone tablets. In this, the author rejoins the teaching of Paul in Romans 7-8.³ The corollary is that the hearers of the letter had better understand that they ought to be "perfect" (*teleioi*) just as their high priest is:

> For it was fitting that he, for whom and by whom all things exist, in bringing many sons to glory, should *make* the pioneer of their salvation *perfect* (*teleiōsai*) through suffering ... Although he was a Son, he learned obedience through what he suffered; and being *made perfect* (*teleiōtheis*) he became the source of eternal salvation to all who obey him, being designated by God a high priest after the order of Melchizedek ... But solid food is for the mature (*teleiōn*), for those who have their faculties trained by practice to distinguish good from evil. Therefore let us leave the elementary doctrine of Christ and go on to maturity (*teleiotēta*). (Heb 2:10; 5:8-10; 5:14-6:1)

This call to "perfection" is corroborated by what was written in chapter 7 concerning the first issuance of the Law and the priestly service related to it: "Now if perfection (*teleiōsis*) had been attainable through the Levitical priesthood (for under it the people received the law [*nenomothetētai*]),⁴ what further need would there have been for another priest to arise after the order of Melchizedek, rather than one named after the order of Aaron?" (v.11) The service of the "true tent," which is the heavenly as well as original one, to which Christ is assigned in the latter days, could not possibly be but perfect. It is the ministry of its copy that is found wanting due to the sins of the people.

---

³ See my comments earlier on Heb 6:1a: "Therefore let us leave the elementary doctrine of Christ and go on to maturity."
⁴ The same verb found in 8:6.

Teaching under the new covenant

There seems to be a contradiction between the non-necessity of teaching one another in the new covenant (Heb 8:11; Jer 31:34) and the importance given teachers at the end of the letter: "Remember your leaders, those who spoke to you the word of God; consider the outcome of their life, and imitate their faith … Obey your leaders and submit to them; for they are keeping watch over your souls, as men who will have to give account. Let them do this joyfully, and not sadly, for that would be of no advantage to you." (Heb 13:7, 17) However, this apparent contradiction is clarified when the new covenant is correctly understood.

The new covenant, as underscored earlier, is *not* law-less, that is to say without law. It upholds the *same* statutes governing the old covenant. Now, however, this law is written on the heart (Heb 8:10; Jer 31:33) rather than on tablets of stone. In other words, the intent of the law is not so much to have its commandments mentally known and memorized as it is for them to be executed. This is evident from the repeated summons "to do them" in Deuteronomy:

> And now, O Israel, give heed to the statutes and the ordinances which I teach you, and do them; that you may live, and go in and take possession of the land which the Lord, the God of your fathers, gives you. (4:1)

> Behold, I have taught you statutes and ordinances, as the Lord my God commanded me, that you should do them in the land which you are entering to take possession of it. (4:5)

> And the Lord commanded me at that time to teach you statutes and ordinances, that you might do them in the land which you are going over to possess. (4:14)

And Moses summoned all Israel, and said to them, "Hear, O Israel, the statutes and the ordinances which I speak in your hearing this day, and you shall learn them and be careful to do them." (5:1)

But you, stand here by me, and I will tell you all the commandment and the statutes and the ordinances which you shall teach them, that they may do them in the land which I give them to possess. (5:31)

Now this is the commandment, the statutes and the ordinances which the Lord your God commanded me to teach you, that you may do them in the land to which you are going over, to possess it. (6:1)

Hear therefore, O Israel, and be careful to do them; that it may go well with you, and that you may multiply greatly, as the Lord, the God of your fathers, has promised you, in a land flowing with milk and honey. (6:3)

And because you hearken to these ordinances, and keep and do them, the Lord your God will keep with you the covenant and the steadfast love which he swore to your fathers to keep. (7:12)

This day the Lord your God commands you to do these statutes and ordinances; you shall therefore be careful to do them with all your heart and with all your soul. (26:16)

And the Lord will make you the head, and not the tail; and you shall tend upward only, and not downward; if you obey the commandments of the Lord your God, which I command you this day, being careful to do them, (28:13)

he [Moses] said to them, "Lay to heart all the words which I enjoin upon you this day, that you may command them to your children, that they may be careful to do all the words of this law." (32:46)

Consequently, when the law is a text written "on stones," to which the elder is privy, he teaches the younger *out of* the written text, in order for the younger *to do* what is taught. When the law is written on the hearts, the teaching consists of reminding the hearers of that *writ*, that is, reminding them of what they already know, in order for them *to do* accordingly. This is precisely what one hears in Paul's admonition to the bishop Timothy, the teacher par excellence in the church:

> Command and teach these things. Let no one despise your youth, but set the believers an example in speech and conduct, in love, in faith, in purity. Till I come, attend to *the public reading of scripture*, to preaching, to teaching. Do not neglect the gift you have, which was given you by prophetic utterance when the council of elders laid their hands upon you. Practice these duties, devote yourself to them, so that all may see your progress. Take heed to yourself and to your teaching; hold to that, for by so doing you will save both yourself and your hearers. (1 Tim 4:11-16)

And if Timothy is able to preach and teach, that is to say, remind his hearers of the content of scripture, it is because "from childhood you have been acquainted with the sacred writings which are able to instruct you for salvation through faith in Christ Jesus. All scripture is inspired by God and profitable for teaching, for reproof, for correction, and for training in righteousness" (2 Tim 3:15-16).

Chapter 9

Vv. 9:1-28 ¹Εἶχε μὲν οὖν [καὶ] ἡ πρώτη δικαιώματα λατρείας τό τε ἅγιον κοσμικόν. ²σκηνὴ γὰρ κατεσκευάσθη ἡ πρώτη ἐν ᾗ ἥ τε λυχνία καὶ ἡ τράπεζα καὶ ἡ πρόθεσις τῶν ἄρτων, ἥτις λέγεται Ἅγια· ³μετὰ δὲ τὸ δεύτερον καταπέτασμα σκηνὴ ἡ λεγομένη Ἅγια Ἁγίων, ⁴χρυσοῦν ἔχουσα θυμιατήριον καὶ τὴν κιβωτὸν τῆς διαθήκης περικεκαλυμμένην πάντοθεν χρυσίῳ, ἐν ᾗ στάμνος χρυσῆ ἔχουσα τὸ μάννα καὶ ἡ ῥάβδος Ἀαρὼν ἡ βλαστήσασα καὶ αἱ πλάκες τῆς διαθήκης, ⁵ὑπεράνω δὲ αὐτῆς Χερουβὶν δόξης κατασκιάζοντα τὸ ἱλαστήριον· περὶ ὧν οὐκ ἔστιν νῦν λέγειν κατὰ μέρος. ⁶Τούτων δὲ οὕτως κατεσκευασμένων εἰς μὲν τὴν πρώτην σκηνὴν διὰ παντὸς εἰσίασιν οἱ ἱερεῖς τὰς λατρείας ἐπιτελοῦντες, ⁷εἰς δὲ τὴν δευτέραν ἅπαξ τοῦ ἐνιαυτοῦ μόνος ὁ ἀρχιερεύς, οὐ χωρὶς αἵματος ὃ προσφέρει ὑπὲρ ἑαυτοῦ καὶ τῶν τοῦ λαοῦ ἀγνοημάτων, ⁸τοῦτο δηλοῦντος τοῦ πνεύματος τοῦ ἁγίου, μήπω πεφανερῶσθαι τὴν τῶν ἁγίων ὁδὸν ἔτι τῆς πρώτης σκηνῆς ἐχούσης στάσιν, ⁹ἥτις παραβολὴ εἰς τὸν καιρὸν τὸν ἐνεστηκότα, καθ᾽ ἣν δῶρά τε καὶ θυσίαι προσφέρονται μὴ δυνάμεναι κατὰ συνείδησιν τελειῶσαι τὸν λατρεύοντα, ¹⁰μόνον ἐπὶ βρώμασιν καὶ πόμασιν καὶ διαφόροις βαπτισμοῖς, δικαιώματα σαρκὸς μέχρι καιροῦ διορθώσεως ἐπικείμενα. ¹¹Χριστὸς δὲ παραγενόμενος ἀρχιερεὺς τῶν γενομένων ἀγαθῶν διὰ τῆς μείζονος καὶ τελειοτέρας σκηνῆς οὐ χειροποιήτου, τοῦτ᾽ ἔστιν οὐ ταύτης τῆς κτίσεως, ¹²οὐδὲ δι᾽ αἵματος τράγων καὶ μόσχων διὰ δὲ τοῦ ἰδίου αἵματος εἰσῆλθεν ἐφάπαξ εἰς τὰ ἅγια αἰωνίαν λύτρωσιν εὑράμενος. ¹³εἰ γὰρ τὸ αἷμα τράγων καὶ ταύρων καὶ σποδὸς δαμάλεως ῥαντίζουσα τοὺς κεκοινωμένους ἁγιάζει πρὸς τὴν τῆς σαρκὸς καθαρότητα, ¹⁴πόσῳ μᾶλλον τὸ αἷμα τοῦ Χριστοῦ, ὃς διὰ πνεύματος αἰωνίου ἑαυτὸν προσήνεγκεν ἄμωμον τῷ θεῷ, καθαριεῖ τὴν συνείδησιν ἡμῶν ἀπὸ νεκρῶν ἔργων εἰς τὸ λατρεύειν θεῷ ζῶντι. ¹⁵Καὶ διὰ τοῦτο διαθήκης καινῆς μεσίτης ἐστίν, ὅπως θανάτου γενομένου εἰς ἀπολύτρωσιν τῶν ἐπὶ τῇ πρώτῃ διαθήκῃ παραβάσεων τὴν ἐπαγγελίαν λάβωσιν οἱ κεκλημένοι τῆς αἰωνίου κληρονομίας. ¹⁶ Ὅπου γὰρ διαθήκη, θάνατον ἀνάγκη φέρεσθαι τοῦ διαθεμένου· ¹⁷διαθήκη γὰρ ἐπὶ νεκροῖς βεβαία, ἐπεὶ μήποτε ἰσχύει ὅτε ζῇ ὁ διαθέμενος. ¹⁸ὅθεν οὐδὲ ἡ πρώτη χωρὶς αἵματος ἐγκεκαίνισται· ¹⁹λαληθείσης γὰρ πάσης ἐντολῆς κατὰ τὸν νόμον ὑπὸ Μωϋσέως παντὶ τῷ λαῷ, λαβὼν τὸ αἷμα τῶν μόσχων [καὶ τῶν τράγων] μετὰ ὕδατος καὶ ἐρίου κοκκίνου καὶ ὑσσώπου αὐτό τε τὸ βιβλίον καὶ πάντα τὸν λαὸν ἐρράντισεν ²⁰λέγων· τοῦτο τὸ αἷμα τῆς διαθήκης ἧς ἐνετείλατο πρὸς ὑμᾶς ὁ θεός. ²¹καὶ τὴν σκηνὴν δὲ καὶ πάντα τὰ σκεύη τῆς λειτουργίας τῷ αἵματι ὁμοίως ἐρράντισεν. ²² καὶ σχεδὸν ἐν αἵματι πάντα καθαρίζεται κατὰ τὸν νόμον καὶ χωρὶς αἱματεκχυσίας οὐ γίνεται ἄφεσις. ²³ Ἀνάγκη οὖν τὰ μὲν ὑποδείγματα τῶν ἐν τοῖς οὐρανοῖς τούτοις καθαρίζεσθαι, αὐτὰ δὲ τὰ ἐπουράνια κρείττοσιν θυσίαις παρὰ ταύτας. ²⁴οὐ γὰρ εἰς χειροποίητα εἰσῆλθεν ἅγια Χριστός, ἀντίτυπα τῶν ἀληθινῶν, ἀλλ' εἰς αὐτὸν τὸν οὐρανόν, νῦν ἐμφανισθῆναι τῷ προσώπῳ τοῦ θεοῦ ὑπὲρ ἡμῶν· ²⁵οὐδ' ἵνα πολλάκις προσφέρῃ ἑαυτόν, ὥσπερ ὁ ἀρχιερεὺς εἰσέρχεται εἰς τὰ ἅγια κατ' ἐνιαυτὸν ἐν αἵματι ἀλλοτρίῳ, ²⁶ἐπεὶ ἔδει αὐτὸν πολλάκις παθεῖν ἀπὸ καταβολῆς κόσμου· νυνὶ δὲ ἅπαξ ἐπὶ συντελείᾳ τῶν αἰώνων εἰς ἀθέτησιν [τῆς] ἁμαρτίας διὰ τῆς θυσίας αὐτοῦ πεφανέρωται. ²⁷καὶ καθ' ὅσον ἀπόκειται τοῖς ἀνθρώποις ἅπαξ ἀποθανεῖν, μετὰ δὲ τοῦτο κρίσις, ²⁸οὕτως καὶ ὁ Χριστὸς ἅπαξ προσενεχθεὶς εἰς τὸ πολλῶν ἀνενεγκεῖν ἁμαρτίας ἐκ δευτέρου χωρὶς ἁμαρτίας ὀφθήσεται τοῖς αὐτὸν ἀπεκδεχομένοις εἰς σωτηρίαν.

¹Now even the first covenant had regulations for worship and an earthly sanctuary. ²For a tent was prepared, the outer one, in which were the lampstand and the table and the bread of the Presence; it is called the Holy Place. ³Behind the second curtain stood a tent called the Holy of Holies, ⁴having the golden altar of incense and the ark of the covenant covered on all sides with gold, which contained a golden urn holding the manna, and Aaron's rod that budded, and the tables of the covenant; ⁵above it were the cherubim of glory overshadowing the mercy seat. Of these things we cannot now speak in detail. ⁶These preparations having thus been made, the priests go continually into the outer tent, performing their ritual duties; ⁷but into the second only the high priest goes, and he but once a year, and not without taking blood which he offers for himself and for the errors of the people.

⁸By this the Holy Spirit indicates that the way into the sanctuary is not yet opened as long as the outer tent is still standing ⁹(which is symbolic for the present age). According to this arrangement, gifts and sacrifices are offered which cannot perfect the conscience of the worshiper, ¹⁰but deal only with food and drink and various ablutions, regulations for the body imposed until the time of reformation. ¹¹But when Christ appeared as a high priest of the good things that have come, then through the greater and more perfect tent (not made with hands, that is, not of this creation) ¹²he entered once for all into the Holy Place, taking not the blood of goats and calves but his own blood, thus securing an eternal redemption. ¹³For if the sprinkling of defiled persons with the blood of goats and bulls and with the ashes of a heifer sanctifies for the purification of the flesh, ¹⁴how much more shall the blood of Christ, who through the eternal Spirit offered himself without blemish to God, purify your conscience from dead works to serve the living God. ¹⁵Therefore he is the mediator of a new covenant, so that those who are called may receive the promised eternal inheritance, since a death has occurred which redeems them from the transgressions under the first covenant. ¹⁶For where a will is involved, the death of the one who made it must be established. ¹⁷For a will takes effect only at death, since it is not in force as long as the one who made it is alive. ¹⁸Hence even the first covenant was not ratified without blood. ¹⁹For when every commandment of the law had been declared by Moses to all the people, he took the blood of calves and goats, with water and scarlet wool and hyssop, and sprinkled both the book itself and all the people, ²⁰saying, "This is the blood of the covenant which God commanded you." ²¹And in the same way he sprinkled with the blood both the tent and all the vessels used in worship. ²²Indeed, under the law almost everything is purified with blood, and without the shedding of blood there is no forgiveness of sins. ²³Thus it was necessary for

> the copies of the heavenly things to be purified with these rites, but the heavenly things themselves with better sacrifices than these. ²⁴For Christ has entered, not into a sanctuary made with hands, a copy of the true one, but into heaven itself, now to appear in the presence of God on our behalf. ²⁵Nor was it to offer himself repeatedly, as the high priest enters the Holy Place yearly with blood not his own; ²⁶for then he would have had to suffer repeatedly since the foundation of the world. But as it is, he has appeared once for all at the end of the age to put away sin by the sacrifice of himself. ²⁷And just as it is appointed for men to die once, and after that comes judgment, ²⁸so Christ, having been offered once to bear the sins of many, will appear a second time, not to deal with sin but to save those who are eagerly waiting for him.

In classical theology, the heavenly and earthly realms are usually perceived as "up above" and "down here" realities. Thus when hearing Hebrews 9 most of us perceive the heavenly sanctuary or tent as a "mystical" ever-present reality that may be revealed to us, or to which we can be privy at a moment of "ecstasy" during our earthly life. This, however, is not the reality of the matter in scripture. The heavenly tent is either behind us or ahead of us. Only Moses was privy to its vision while on the mountain, and the only one who actually entered it was Christ. The rest of us *await* its descent at Christ's *coming* (Rev 21:1-2) or at his "appearance" *a second time* (Heb 9:28). The emphasis on the coming Jerusalem is confirmed by the use of the noun *diorthōseōs*, which is unique in scripture: "According to this arrangement, gifts and sacrifices are offered which cannot perfect the conscience of the worshiper, but deal only with food and drink and various ablutions, regulations for the body imposed until the time of reformation (*diorthōseōs*)." (vv.9b-10) This is an obvious reference to the new Jerusalem in Isaiah:

For Zion's sake I will not keep silent, and for Jerusalem's sake I will not rest, until her vindication goes forth as brightness, and her salvation as a burning torch. The nations shall see your vindication, and all the kings your glory; and you shall be called by a new name which the mouth of the Lord will give. You shall be a crown of beauty in the hand of the Lord, and a royal diadem in the hand of your God. You shall no more be termed Forsaken, and your land shall no more be termed Desolate; but you shall be called My delight is in her, and your land Married; for the Lord delights in you, and your land shall be married. For as a young man marries a virgin, so shall your sons marry you, and as the bridegroom rejoices over the bride, so shall your God rejoice over you. Upon your walls, O Jerusalem, I have set watchmen; all the day and all the night they shall never be silent. You who put the Lord in remembrance, take no rest, and give him no rest until he establishes (diorthōsē; reforms) Jerusalem and makes it a praise in the earth. The Lord has sworn by his right hand and by his mighty arm: "I will not again give your grain to be food for your enemies, and foreigners shall not drink your wine for which you have labored; but those who garner it shall eat it and praise the Lord, and those who gather it shall drink it in the courts of my sanctuary (tais hagiais).[1]" (62:1-9)

---

[1] Literally, "the holy things." This is the same expression the author of Hebrews used earlier to refer to the sanctuary: "Now the point in what we are saying is this: we have such a high priest, one who is seated at the right hand of the throne of the Majesty in heaven, a minister in the sanctuary (*tōn hagiōn*) and the true tent which is set up not by man but by the Lord" (Heb 8:1-2); "By this the Holy Spirit indicates that the way into the sanctuary (*tōn hagiōn*) is not yet opened as long as the outer tent is still standing." (9:8)

In the Septuagint, the connotation and novelty of reformation is conveyed by the rare usage of verbs from the root *diorthō*: "Thus says the Lord of hosts, the God of Israel, Amend (*diorthōsate*) your ways and your doings, and I will let you dwell in this place ... For if you truly (*diorthountes*; amending) amend (*diorthōsēte*) your ways and your doings, if you truly execute justice one with another..." (Jer 7:3, 5)

What applies to the new Zion and its sanctuary also applies to Christ. In other words, as the heavenly emissary, Christ is either behind us through his teaching or ahead of us as the judge who will determine whether or not we have hearkened to that teaching: "so Christ, having been offered once to bear the sins of many, will appear a second time, not to deal with sin but to save those who are eagerly waiting (*apekdekhomenois*) for him." (Heb 9:28) Using metaphorical terminology, heavenly realities in scripture are "above" but at a slant, that is, at an angle, making them never at our fingertips. In other words, either we "reminisce" about the heavenly teaching as manna *in the wilderness*, or we faithfully "await" and "hope" that we would be "saved" or "rescued" from the "coming wrath": "For they themselves report concerning us what a welcome we had among you, and how you turned to God from idols, to *serve* (*doulevein*) a *living* and true *God* (*Theō zōnti*), and to wait for his Son from heaven, whom he raised from the dead, Jesus who delivers us from the wrath to come." (1 Thess 1:9-10) This statement influenced Hebrews 9:14: "how much more shall the blood of Christ, who through the eternal Spirit offered himself without blemish to God, purify your conscience from dead works to *serve* (*latrevein*)[2] the living God (*Theō zōnti*)." On the other hand,

---

[2] Both *doulevein* and *latrevein* are from the same original Hebrew *'abad* (serve, worship).

apekdekhomenois (eagerly waiting) is vintage Pauline and systematically refers to something "coming":

> I consider that the sufferings of this present time are not worth comparing with the glory that is to be revealed to us. For the creation waits with eager longing (*apekdekhetai*) for the revealing of the sons of God; for the creation was subjected to futility, not of its own will but by the will of him who subjected it in hope; because the creation itself will be set free from its bondage to decay and obtain the glorious liberty of the children of God. We know that the whole creation has been groaning in travail together until now; and not only the creation, but we ourselves, who have the first fruits of the Spirit, groan inwardly as we wait (*apekdekhomenoi*) for adoption as sons, the redemption of our bodies. For in this hope we were saved. Now hope that is seen is not hope. For who hopes for what he sees? But if we hope for what we do not see, we wait (*apekdekhometha*) for it with patience. (Rom 8:18-25)

> I give thanks to God always for you because of the grace of God which was given you in Christ Jesus, that in every way you were enriched in him with all speech and all knowledge—even as the testimony to Christ was confirmed among you—so that you are not lacking in any spiritual gift, as you wait (*apekdekhomenous*) for the revealing of our Lord Jesus Christ; who will sustain you to the end, guiltless in the day of our Lord Jesus Christ. God is faithful, by whom you were called into the fellowship of his Son, Jesus Christ our Lord. (1 Cor 1:4-9)

> For through the Spirit, by faith, we wait (*apekdekhometha*) for the hope of righteousness. (Gal 5:5)

> But our commonwealth is in heaven, and from it we await (*apekdekhometha*) a Savior, the Lord Jesus Christ, who will change

our lowly body to be like his glorious body, by the power which enables him even to subject all things to himself. (Phil 3:20-21)[3]

So, all in all, Hebrews 9 functions much the same as 1 Corinthians 15; that is, it is not so much a treatise about the resurrection, but an assuredness that all, living or dead, will undergo the final judgment.[4] It is not so much a description of the heavenly tent where the hearers are headed, but rather it is the place where only Christ already resides "seated at the right hand of the throne of the Majesty" (Heb 8:2). The hearers are invited to share the tent with him on the condition that they abide by his teaching concerning their daily behavior *on their way* toward the heavenly Zion.

Three features of chapter 9 militate for the correctness of this understanding. First, it is replete with Pauline terminology that reflects divine judgment. Besides the verb *apekdekhomai* and "the time of reformation," one will notice the following:

1. V.9:9b: "According to this arrangement, gifts and sacrifices are offered which cannot perfect (*teleiōsai*) the conscience (*syneidēsin*) of the worshiper." Both "perfection" (maturity) and "conscience" are staple elements in the Pauline letters.[5]

---

[3] The only other occurrence of that verb in the New Testament is found in 1 Pet 3:20 to depict God's patience at the time of the flood: "[the dead] who formerly did not obey, when God's patience waited (*apekdekheto*) in the days of Noah, during the building of the ark, in which a few, that is, eight persons, were saved through water."

[4] See my detailed comments in *C-1Cor* 259-95.

[5] See Rom 12:2; 1 Cor 2:6; 13:10; 14:20; Gal 3:3; Eph 4:13; Phil 3:12, 15; Col 1:28; 3:14; 4:12 for the root *teleio*— and Rom 2:15; 9:1; 13:5; 1 Cor 8:7, 10, 12; 10:25, 27, 28, 29 [twice]; 2 Cor 1:12; 4:2; 5:11; 1 Tim 1:5, 19; 3:9; 4:2; 2 Tim 1:3; Tit 1:15 for "conscience."

2. V. 14: "how much more shall the blood of Christ, who through the eternal Spirit offered himself without blemish (*amōmon*) to God, purify (*kathariei*) your conscience from dead works (*nekrōn ergōn*) to *serve the living God*." This is an echo of the Pauline teaching.

3. Vv. 14-15, "Redemption (*apolytrōsin*) from transgressions (*parabaseōn*) through the blood of Christ, as mediator (*mesitēs*), unto the promised inheritance" recall Ephesians 1:7, 14, "In him we have redemption through his blood, the forgiveness of our trespasses (*paraptōmatōn*),[6] according to the riches of his grace ... Which is the earnest of our inheritance until the redemption of the purchased possession, unto the praise of his glory." These verses also echo Galatians 3:18-20, "For if the inheritance is by the law, it is no longer by promise; but God gave it to Abraham by a promise. Why then the law? It was added because of transgressions, till the offspring should come to whom the promise had been made; and it was ordained by angels through an intermediary (*mesitou*). Now an intermediary (*mesitēs*) implies more than one; but God is one."[7]

Secondly, the author's choice of *dikaiōmata* used twice to refer to the Law's regulations (Heb 9:1, 10) is clearly intentional since these are the only instances of that noun in the letter. The

---

[6] *parabaseōn* and *paraptōmatōn* carry practically the same connotation of "sinning" against the commandments of the Law.

[7] Outside Gal 3:19, 20 and Heb 8:6; 9:15; 12:24, *mesitēs* occurs only in 1 Tim 2:5.

addressees are reminded that righteousness (*dikaiosynē*) remains the issue. They will soon be hearing that unless one is righteous, one shall not inherit life in the eternal city:

> Therefore do not throw away your confidence, which has a great reward. For you have need of endurance, so that you may do the will of God and receive what is promised. "For yet a little while, and the coming one shall come and shall not tarry; but my righteous one shall live by faith, and if he shrinks back, my soul has no pleasure in him." But we are not of those who shrink back and are destroyed, but of those who have faith and keep their souls. (10:35-39)

Finally, and perhaps most importantly, it is the author's use of "tent" that is striking. Outside of Hebrews in the New Testament, reference to the tent of witness is confined to Acts 7:44 and Revelation 15:5. This opening reference to the "tent" (Heb 8:2) sets the tone for its meaning and function in the rest of the letter. The nine incidences of "tent" in Hebrews top the seven instances of "sanctuary." Underscoring the mobility of the divine residence that hosts the words of the Law is to remind the hearers that their situation is similar to that of their forebears. While in the wilderness the tent led the way and, by extension, was leading them *on the way* to the inheritance and (place of) rest that always was *ahead*. In other words, one does not "mystically" ascend to "the true tent which is set up not by man but by the Lord" (Heb 8:2); one follows the "way" leading to it, which is none other than the "way" set according to the Pauline gospel:

> Therefore, brethren, since we have confidence to enter the sanctuary by the blood of Jesus, by the new and living way which he opened for us through the curtain, that is, through his flesh, and since we have a great priest over the house of God, let us draw near with a true heart in full assurance of faith, with our

hearts sprinkled clean from an evil conscience and our bodies washed with pure water. Let us hold fast the confession of our hope without wavering, for he who promised is faithful; and let us consider how to stir up one another to love and good works, not neglecting to meet together, as is the habit of some, but encouraging one another, and all the more as you see the Day drawing near. (10:19-25)

Chapter 10

Vv. 10:1-39 ¹Σκιὰν γὰρ ἔχων ὁ νόμος τῶν μελλόντων ἀγαθῶν, οὐκ αὐτὴν τὴν εἰκόνα τῶν πραγμάτων, κατ᾽ ἐνιαυτὸν ταῖς αὐταῖς θυσίαις ἃς προσφέρουσιν εἰς τὸ διηνεκὲς οὐδέποτε δύναται τοὺς προσερχομένους τελειῶσαι· ²ἐπεὶ οὐκ ἂν ἐπαύσαντο προσφερόμεναι διὰ τὸ μηδεμίαν ἔχειν ἔτι συνείδησιν ἁμαρτιῶν τοὺς λατρεύοντας ἅπαξ κεκαθαρισμένους; ³ἀλλ᾽ ἐν αὐταῖς ἀνάμνησις ἁμαρτιῶν κατ᾽ ἐνιαυτόν· ⁴ἀδύνατον γὰρ αἷμα ταύρων καὶ τράγων ἀφαιρεῖν ἁμαρτίας. ⁵Διὸ εἰσερχόμενος εἰς τὸν κόσμον λέγει· θυσίαν καὶ προσφορὰν οὐκ ἠθέλησας, σῶμα δὲ κατηρτίσω μοι· ⁶ὁλοκαυτώματα καὶ περὶ ἁμαρτίας οὐκ εὐδόκησας. ⁷τότε εἶπον· ἰδοὺ ἥκω, ἐν κεφαλίδι βιβλίου γέγραπται περὶ ἐμοῦ, τοῦ ποιῆσαι ὁ θεὸς τὸ θέλημά σου. ⁸ἀνώτερον λέγων ὅτι θυσίας καὶ προσφορὰς καὶ ὁλοκαυτώματα καὶ περὶ ἁμαρτίας οὐκ ἠθέλησας οὐδὲ εὐδόκησας, αἵτινες κατὰ νόμον προσφέρονται, ⁹τότε εἴρηκεν· ἰδοὺ ἥκω τοῦ ποιῆσαι τὸ θέλημά σου. ἀναιρεῖ τὸ πρῶτον ἵνα τὸ δεύτερον στήσῃ, ¹⁰ἐν ᾧ θελήματι ἡγιασμένοι ἐσμὲν διὰ τῆς προσφορᾶς τοῦ σώματος Ἰησοῦ Χριστοῦ ἐφάπαξ. ¹¹Καὶ πᾶς μὲν ἱερεὺς ἕστηκεν καθ᾽ ἡμέραν λειτουργῶν καὶ τὰς αὐτὰς πολλάκις προσφέρων θυσίας, αἵτινες οὐδέποτε δύνανται περιελεῖν ἁμαρτίας, ¹²οὗτος δὲ μίαν ὑπὲρ ἁμαρτιῶν προσενέγκας θυσίαν εἰς τὸ διηνεκὲς ἐκάθισεν ἐν δεξιᾷ τοῦ θεοῦ, ¹³τὸ λοιπὸν ἐκδεχόμενος ἕως τεθῶσιν οἱ ἐχθροὶ αὐτοῦ ὑποπόδιον τῶν ποδῶν αὐτοῦ. ¹⁴μιᾷ γὰρ προσφορᾷ τετελείωκεν εἰς τὸ διηνεκὲς τοὺς ἁγιαζομένους. ¹⁵Μαρτυρεῖ δὲ ἡμῖν καὶ τὸ πνεῦμα τὸ ἅγιον· μετὰ γὰρ τὸ εἰρηκέναι· ¹⁶αὕτη ἡ διαθήκη ἣν διαθήσομαι πρὸς αὐτοὺς μετὰ τὰς ἡμέρας ἐκείνας, λέγει κύριος· διδοὺς νόμους μου ἐπὶ καρδίας αὐτῶν καὶ ἐπὶ τὴν διάνοιαν αὐτῶν ἐπιγράψω αὐτούς, ¹⁷καὶ τῶν ἁμαρτιῶν αὐτῶν καὶ τῶν ἀνομιῶν αὐτῶν οὐ μὴ μνησθήσομαι ἔτι. ¹⁸ὅπου δὲ ἄφεσις τούτων, οὐκέτι προσφορὰ περὶ ἁμαρτίας. ¹⁹Ἔχοντες οὖν, ἀδελφοί, παρρησίαν εἰς τὴν εἴσοδον τῶν ἁγίων ἐν τῷ αἵματι Ἰησοῦ, ²⁰ἣν ἐνεκαίνισεν ἡμῖν ὁδὸν πρόσφατον καὶ ζῶσαν διὰ τοῦ καταπετάσματος, τοῦτ᾽ ἔστιν τῆς σαρκὸς αὐτοῦ, ²¹καὶ ἱερέα μέγαν ἐπὶ τὸν οἶκον τοῦ θεοῦ, ²²προσερχώμεθα μετὰ ἀληθινῆς καρδίας ἐν πληροφορίᾳ πίστεως ῥεραντισμένοι τὰς καρδίας ἀπὸ συνειδήσεως πονηρᾶς καὶ λελουσμένοι τὸ σῶμα ὕδατι καθαρῷ· ²³κατέχωμεν τὴν ὁμολογίαν τῆς ἐλπίδος ἀκλινῆ, πιστὸς γὰρ ὁ ἐπαγγειλάμενος, ²⁴καὶ κατανοῶμεν ἀλλήλους εἰς παροξυσμὸν ἀγάπης καὶ καλῶν ἔργων, ²⁵μὴ ἐγκαταλείποντες τὴν ἐπισυναγωγὴν ἑαυτῶν, καθὼς ἔθος τισίν, ἀλλὰ παρακαλοῦντες, καὶ τοσούτῳ μᾶλλον ὅσῳ βλέπετε ἐγγίζουσαν τὴν ἡμέραν. ²⁶ Ἑκουσίως γὰρ ἁμαρτανόντων ἡμῶν μετὰ τὸ λαβεῖν τὴν ἐπίγνωσιν τῆς ἀληθείας, οὐκέτι περὶ ἁμαρτιῶν ἀπολείπεται θυσία, ²⁷φοβερὰ δέ τις ἐκδοχὴ κρίσεως καὶ πυρὸς ζῆλος ἐσθίειν μέλλοντος τοὺς ὑπεναντίους. ²⁸ἀθετήσας τις νόμον Μωϋσέως χωρὶς οἰκτιρμῶν ἐπὶ δυσὶν ἢ τρισὶν μάρτυσιν ἀποθνῄσκει· ²⁹πόσῳ δοκεῖτε χείρονος ἀξιωθήσεται τιμωρίας ὁ τὸν υἱὸν τοῦ θεοῦ καταπατήσας καὶ τὸ αἷμα τῆς διαθήκης κοινὸν ἡγησάμενος, ἐν ᾧ ἡγιάσθη, καὶ τὸ πνεῦμα τῆς χάριτος ἐνυβρίσας; ³⁰οἴδαμεν γὰρ τὸν εἰπόντα· ἐμοὶ ἐκδίκησις, ἐγὼ ἀνταποδώσω. καὶ πάλιν· κρινεῖ κύριος τὸν λαὸν αὐτοῦ. ³¹φοβερὸν τὸ ἐμπεσεῖν εἰς χεῖρας θεοῦ ζῶντος. ³² Ἀναμιμνῄσκεσθε δὲ τὰς πρότερον ἡμέρας, ἐν αἷς φωτισθέντες πολλὴν ἄθλησιν ὑπεμείνατε παθημάτων, ³³τοῦτο μὲν ὀνειδισμοῖς τε καὶ θλίψεσιν θεατριζόμενοι, τοῦτο δὲ κοινωνοὶ τῶν οὕτως ἀναστρεφομένων γενηθέντες. ³⁴καὶ γὰρ τοῖς δεσμίοις συνεπαθήσατε καὶ τὴν ἁρπαγὴν τῶν ὑπαρχόντων ὑμῶν μετὰ χαρᾶς προσεδέξασθε γινώσκοντες ἔχειν ἑαυτοὺς κρείττονα ὕπαρξιν καὶ μένουσαν. ³⁵Μὴ ἀποβάλητε οὖν τὴν παρρησίαν ὑμῶν, ἥτις ἔχει μεγάλην μισθαποδοσίαν. ³⁶ὑπομονῆς γὰρ ἔχετε χρείαν ἵνα τὸ θέλημα τοῦ θεοῦ ποιήσαντες κομίσησθε τὴν ἐπαγγελίαν. ³⁷ἔτι γὰρ μικρὸν ὅσον ὅσον, ὁ ἐρχόμενος ἥξει καὶ οὐ χρονίσει· ³⁸ὁ δὲ δίκαιός μου ἐκ πίστεως ζήσεται, καὶ ἐὰν ὑποστείληται, οὐκ εὐδοκεῖ ἡ ψυχή μου ἐν αὐτῷ. ³⁹ἡμεῖς δὲ οὐκ ἐσμὲν ὑποστολῆς εἰς ἀπώλειαν ἀλλὰ πίστεως εἰς περιποίησιν ψυχῆς.

¹For since the law has but a shadow of the good things to come instead of the true form of these realities, it can never, by the same sacrifices which are continually offered year after year, make perfect those who draw near. ²Otherwise, would they not have ceased to be offered? If the worshipers had once been cleansed, they would no longer have any consciousness of sin. ³But in these sacrifices there is a reminder of sin year after year. ⁴For it is impossible that the blood of bulls and goats should take away sins. ⁵Consequently, when Christ came into the world, he said, "Sacrifices and offerings thou hast not desired, but a body hast thou prepared for me; [6]in burnt offerings and sin offerings thou hast taken no pleasure. [7]Then I said, 'Lo, I have come to do thy will, O God,' as it is written of me in the roll of the book." [8]When he said above, "Thou hast neither desired nor taken pleasure in sacrifices and offerings and burnt offerings and sin offerings" (these are offered according to the law), [9]then he added, "Lo, I have come to do thy will." He abolishes the first in order to establish the second. [10]And by that will we have been sanctified through the offering of the body of Jesus Christ once for all. [11]And every priest stands daily at his service, offering repeatedly the same sacrifices, which can never take away sins. [12]But when Christ had offered for all time a single sacrifice for sins, he sat down at the right hand of God, [13]then to wait until his enemies should be made a stool for his feet. [14]For by a single offering he has perfected for all time those who are sanctified. [15]And the Holy Spirit also bears witness to us; for after saying, [16]"This is the covenant that I will make with them after those days, says the Lord: I will put my laws on their hearts, and write them on their minds," [17]then he adds, "I will remember their sins and their misdeeds no more." [18]Where there is forgiveness of these, there is no longer any offering for sin. [19]Therefore, brethren, since we have confidence to enter the sanctuary by the blood of Jesus, [20]by the new and living way which he opened for us through the curtain, that is, through his flesh, [21]and since we have a great priest over the house of God, [22]let us draw near with a true heart in full assurance of faith, with our hearts sprinkled clean from an evil conscience and our bodies washed with pure water. [23]Let us hold fast the confession of our hope without wavering, for he who promised is faithful; [24]and let us consider how to stir up one another to love and good works, [25]not neglecting to meet together, as is the habit of some, but encouraging one another, and all the more as you see the Day drawing near. ²⁶*For if we sin deliberately after receiving the knowledge of the truth, there no longer remains a sacrifice for sins,* ²⁷*but a fearful prospect of judgment, and a fury of fire which will consume the adversaries.* ²⁸*A man who has violated the law of Moses dies without mercy at the testimony of two or three witnesses.* ²⁹*How much worse punishment do you think will be deserved by the man who has spurned the Son of God, and profaned the blood of the covenant by which he was sanctified, and outraged the Spirit of grace?* ³⁰*For we know him who said, "Vengeance is mine, I will repay." And again, "The Lord will judge his people."* ³¹*It is a fearful thing to fall into the hands of the living God.* ³²*But recall the former days when, after you were enlightened, you endured a hard struggle with sufferings,* ³³*sometimes being publicly exposed to abuse and affliction, and sometimes being partners with those so treated.* ³⁴*For you had compassion on the prisoners, and you joyfully accepted the plundering of your property, since you knew that you yourselves had a better possession and an abiding one.* ³⁵*Therefore do not throw away your confidence, which has a great reward.* ³⁶*For you have need of endurance, so that you may do the will of God and receive what is promised.* ³⁷*"For yet a little while, and the coming one shall come and shall not tarry;* ³⁸*but my righteous one shall live by faith, and if he shrinks back, my soul has no pleasure in him."* ³⁹*But we are not of those who shrink back and are destroyed, but of those who have faith and keep their souls.*

Chapter 10 corroborates the main point of the argument. The stress is not so much on the sacrifices offered by the priests for the sins of the people, but is on the fact that those sins are tantamount to breaking the divine law. It is not so much that the sacrifices were ineffective per se, rather it is the recurrent obstinacy of the people that made them commit new sins after the earlier ones were forgiven. In the previous chapter the author established that salvation brought about by Christ was carried out by the shedding of blood, as were many of the temple sacrifices, because such was required by the Law. The difference lies in that Christ *did God's will as written in scripture*:

> Consequently, when Christ came into the world, he said, "Sacrifices and offerings thou hast not desired, but a body hast thou prepared for me; in burnt offerings and sin offerings thou hast taken no pleasure. Then I said, 'Lo, I have come to do thy will, O God,' as it is written of me in the roll of the book." (Heb 10:5-7 [Ps 40:6-7])

The author underscores that the novel move from the first situation to the second (Heb 10:9b) was due to Christ's abiding by God's will (v.9a), which was to sanctify us through his obedience until death (v.10; see also Phil 2:8). That is precisely why the Law, which is the actual expression of God's will, could not possibly be abolished:

> Think not that I have come to abolish the law and the prophets; I have come not to abolish them but to fulfil them. For truly, I say to you, till heaven and earth pass away, not an iota, not a dot, will pass from the law until all is accomplished. Whoever then relaxes one of the least of these commandments and teaches men so, shall be called least in the kingdom of heaven; but he who does them and teaches them shall be called great in the kingdom of heaven. For I tell you, unless your righteousness exceeds that of the scribes and Pharisees, you will never enter the kingdom of heaven. (Mt 5:17-20)

> So the law is holy, and the commandment is holy and just and good ... So I find it to be a law that when I want to do right, evil lies close at hand. For I delight in the law of God, in my inmost self, but I see in my members another law at war with the law of

> my mind and making me captive to the law of sin which dwells in my members. Wretched man that I am! Who will deliver me from this body of death? Thanks be to God through Jesus Christ our Lord! So then, I of myself serve the law of God with my mind, but with my flesh I serve the law of sin. There is therefore now no condemnation for those who are in Christ Jesus. For the law of the Spirit of life in Christ Jesus has set me free from the law of sin and death. (Rom 7:12; 7:21-8:2)

That is also why the author of Hebrews insists that the Mosaic law foreshadows the same law written on the hearts, and that the earthly tent is the shadow and reflection of the heavenly sanctuary:

> Now the point in what we are saying is this: we have such a high priest, one who is seated at the right hand of the throne of the Majesty in heaven, a minister in the sanctuary and the true tent which is set up not by man but by the Lord. For every high priest is appointed to offer gifts and sacrifices; hence it is necessary for this priest also to have something to offer. Now if he were on earth, he would not be a priest at all, since there are priests who offer gifts according to the law. They serve a copy (*hypodeigmati*; reflection) and shadow (*skia*) of the heavenly sanctuary; for when Moses was about to erect the tent, he was instructed by God, saying, "See that you make everything according to the pattern which was shown you on the mountain." (8:1-5)

> For since the law has but[1] a shadow (*skia*) of the good things to come instead of the true form of these realities, it can never, by the same sacrifices which are continually offered year after year, make perfect those who draw near. (10:1)

These verses contain the only instances of *skia* in Hebrews, so they are to be understood in the same way. RSV's additional

---

[1] Not in the original.

"but" in 10:1 betrays a bias toward a negative connotation of *skia*. However, such a connotation is contradicted by its function in chapter 8 and by the context of chapter 10. God willed both the tent and the Law. The author elaborated on this in chapter 8 and reminds them of it again in 10:16-17. This explains why he cautions that now there will be a more severe divine judgment than that under the rule of the Mosaic law (vv.26-31). So let the hearers beware and stay the course (vv.31-38), that is to say, "have faith and keep their souls" and not "shrink back" lest they be "destroyed" (v.39).

Chapter 11

Vv. 11:1-40 *¹Ἔστιν δὲ πίστις ἐλπιζομένων ὑπόστασις, πραγμάτων ἔλεγχος οὐ βλεπομένων. ² ἐν ταύτῃ γὰρ ἐμαρτυρήθησαν οἱ πρεσβύτεροι. ³ Πίστει νοοῦμεν κατηρτίσθαι τοὺς αἰῶνας ῥήματι θεοῦ, εἰς τὸ μὴ ἐκ φαινομένων τὸ βλεπόμενον γεγονέναι. ⁴ Πίστει πλείονα θυσίαν Ἄβελ παρὰ Κάϊν προσήνεγκεν τῷ θεῷ, δι᾽ ἧς ἐμαρτυρήθη εἶναι δίκαιος, μαρτυροῦντος ἐπὶ τοῖς δώροις αὐτοῦ τοῦ θεοῦ, καὶ δι᾽ αὐτῆς ἀποθανὼν ἔτι λαλεῖ. ⁵ Πίστει Ἐνὼχ μετετέθη τοῦ μὴ ἰδεῖν θάνατον, καὶ οὐχ ηὑρίσκετο διότι μετέθηκεν αὐτὸν ὁ θεός. πρὸ γὰρ τῆς μεταθέσεως μεμαρτύρηται εὐαρεστηκέναι τῷ θεῷ· ⁶ χωρὶς δὲ πίστεως ἀδύνατον εὐαρεστῆσαι· πιστεῦσαι γὰρ δεῖ τὸν προσερχόμενον τῷ θεῷ ὅτι ἔστιν καὶ τοῖς ἐκζητοῦσιν αὐτὸν μισθαποδότης γίνεται. ⁷ Πίστει χρηματισθεὶς Νῶε περὶ τῶν μηδέπω βλεπομένων, εὐλαβηθεὶς κατεσκεύασεν κιβωτὸν εἰς σωτηρίαν τοῦ οἴκου αὐτοῦ δι᾽ ἧς κατέκρινεν τὸν κόσμον, καὶ τῆς κατὰ πίστιν δικαιοσύνης ἐγένετο κληρονόμος. ⁸ Πίστει καλούμενος Ἀβραὰμ ὑπήκουσεν ἐξελθεῖν εἰς τόπον ὃν ἤμελλεν λαμβάνειν εἰς κληρονομίαν, καὶ ἐξῆλθεν μὴ ἐπιστάμενος ποῦ ἔρχεται. ⁹ Πίστει παρῴκησεν εἰς γῆν τῆς ἐπαγγελίας ὡς ἀλλοτρίαν ἐν σκηναῖς κατοικήσας μετὰ Ἰσαὰκ καὶ Ἰακὼβ τῶν συγκληρονόμων τῆς ἐπαγγελίας τῆς αὐτῆς· ¹⁰ ἐξεδέχετο γὰρ τὴν τοὺς θεμελίους ἔχουσαν πόλιν ἧς τεχνίτης καὶ δημιουργὸς ὁ θεός. ¹¹ Πίστει καὶ αὐτὴ Σάρρα στεῖρα δύναμιν εἰς καταβολὴν σπέρματος ἔλαβεν καὶ παρὰ καιρὸν ἡλικίας, ἐπεὶ πιστὸν ἡγήσατο τὸν ἐπαγγειλάμενον. ¹² διὸ καὶ ἀφ᾽ ἑνὸς ἐγεννήθησαν, καὶ ταῦτα νενεκρωμένου, καθὼς τὰ ἄστρα τοῦ οὐρανοῦ τῷ πλήθει καὶ ὡς ἡ ἄμμος ἡ παρὰ τὸ χεῖλος τῆς θαλάσσης ἡ ἀναρίθμητος. ¹³ Κατὰ πίστιν ἀπέθανον οὗτοι πάντες, μὴ λαβόντες τὰς ἐπαγγελίας ἀλλὰ πόρρωθεν αὐτὰς ἰδόντες καὶ ἀσπασάμενοι καὶ ὁμολογήσαντες ὅτι ξένοι καὶ παρεπίδημοί εἰσιν ἐπὶ τῆς γῆς. ¹⁴ οἱ γὰρ τοιαῦτα λέγοντες ἐμφανίζουσιν ὅτι πατρίδα ἐπιζητοῦσιν. ¹⁵ καὶ εἰ μὲν ἐκείνης ἐμνημόνευον ἀφ᾽ ἧς ἐξέβησαν, εἶχον ἂν καιρὸν ἀνακάμψαι· ¹⁶ νῦν δὲ κρείττονος ὀρέγονται, τοῦτ᾽ ἔστιν ἐπουρανίου. διὸ οὐκ ἐπαισχύνεται αὐτοὺς ὁ θεὸς θεὸς ἐπικαλεῖσθαι αὐτῶν· ἡτοίμασεν γὰρ αὐτοῖς πόλιν. ¹⁷ Πίστει προσενήνοχεν Ἀβραὰμ τὸν Ἰσαὰκ πειραζόμενος καὶ τὸν μονογενῆ* προσέφερεν, ὁ τὰς ἐπαγγελίας ἀναδεξάμενος, ¹⁸ πρὸς ὃν ἐλαλήθη ὅτι ἐν Ἰσαὰκ κληθήσεταί σοι σπέρμα, ¹⁹ λογισάμενος ὅτι καὶ ἐκ νεκρῶν ἐγείρειν δυνατὸς ὁ θεός, ὅθεν αὐτὸν καὶ ἐν παραβολῇ ἐκομίσατο. ²⁰ Πίστει καὶ περὶ μελλόντων εὐλόγησεν Ἰσαὰκ τὸν Ἰακὼβ καὶ τὸν Ἠσαῦ. ²¹ Πίστει Ἰακὼβ ἀποθνῄσκων ἕκαστον τῶν υἱῶν Ἰωσὴφ εὐλόγησεν καὶ προσεκύνησεν ἐπὶ τὸ ἄκρον τῆς ῥάβδου αὐτοῦ. ²² Πίστει Ἰωσὴφ τελευτῶν περὶ τῆς ἐξόδου τῶν υἱῶν Ἰσραὴλ ἐμνημόνευσεν καὶ περὶ τῶν ὀστέων αὐτοῦ ἐνετείλατο. ²³ Πίστει Μωϋσῆς γεννηθεὶς ἐκρύβη τρίμηνον ὑπὸ τῶν πατέρων αὐτοῦ, διότι εἶδον ἀστεῖον τὸ παιδίον καὶ οὐκ ἐφοβήθησαν τὸ διάταγμα τοῦ βασιλέως. ²⁴ Πίστει Μωϋσῆς μέγας γενόμενος ἠρνήσατο λέγεσθαι υἱὸς θυγατρὸς Φαραώ, ²⁵ μᾶλλον ἑλόμενος συγκακουχεῖσθαι τῷ λαῷ τοῦ θεοῦ ἢ πρόσκαιρον ἔχειν ἁμαρτίας ἀπόλαυσιν, ²⁶ μείζονα πλοῦτον ἡγησάμενος τῶν Αἰγύπτου θησαυρῶν τὸν ὀνειδισμὸν τοῦ Χριστοῦ· ἀπέβλεπεν γὰρ εἰς τὴν μισθαποδοσίαν. ²⁷ Πίστει κατέλιπεν Αἴγυπτον μὴ φοβηθεὶς τὸν θυμὸν τοῦ βασιλέως· τὸν γὰρ ἀόρατον ὡς ὁρῶν ἐκαρτέρησεν. ²⁸ Πίστει πεποίηκεν τὸ πάσχα καὶ τὴν πρόσχυσιν τοῦ αἵματος, ἵνα μὴ ὁ ὀλοθρεύων τὰ πρωτότοκα θίγῃ αὐτῶν. ²⁹ Πίστει διέβησαν τὴν ἐρυθρὰν θάλασσαν ὡς διὰ ξηρᾶς γῆς, ἧς πεῖραν λαβόντες οἱ Αἰγύπτιοι κατεπόθησαν. ³⁰ Πίστει τὰ τείχη Ἰεριχὼ ἔπεσαν κυκλωθέντα ἐπὶ ἑπτὰ ἡμέρας. ³¹ Πίστει Ῥαὰβ ἡ πόρνη οὐ συναπώλετο τοῖς ἀπειθήσασιν δεξαμένη τοὺς κατασκόπους μετ᾽ εἰρήνης. ³² Καὶ τί ἔτι λέγω; ἐπιλείψει με γὰρ διηγούμενον ὁ χρόνος περὶ Γεδεών, Βαράκ, Σαμψών, Ἰεφθάε, Δαυίδ τε καὶ Σαμουὴλ καὶ τῶν προφητῶν, ³³ οἳ διὰ πίστεως κατηγωνίσαντο βασιλείας, εἰργάσαντο δικαιοσύνην, ἐπέτυχον ἐπαγγελιῶν, ἔφραξαν στόματα λεόντων, ³⁴ ἔσβεσαν δύναμιν πυρός, ἔφυγον στόματα μαχαίρης, ἐδυναμώθησαν ἀπὸ ἀσθενείας, ἐγενήθησαν ἰσχυροὶ ἐν πολέμῳ, παρεμβολὰς ἔκλιναν ἀλλοτρίων. ³⁵ Ἔλαβον γυναῖκες ἐξ ἀναστάσεως τοὺς νεκροὺς αὐτῶν· ἄλλοι δὲ ἐτυμπανίσθησαν οὐ προσδεξάμενοι τὴν ἀπολύτρωσιν, ἵνα κρείττονος ἀναστάσεως τύχωσιν· ³⁶ ἕτεροι δὲ ἐμπαιγμῶν καὶ μαστίγων πεῖραν ἔλαβον, ἔτι δὲ δεσμῶν καὶ φυλακῆς· ³⁷ ἐλιθάσθησαν, ἐπρίσθησαν, ἐν φόνῳ μαχαίρης ἀπέθανον, περιῆλθον ἐν μηλωταῖς, ἐν αἰγείοις δέρμασιν, ὑστερούμενοι, θλιβόμενοι, κακουχούμενοι, ³⁸ ὧν οὐκ ἦν ἄξιος ὁ κόσμος, ἐπὶ ἐρημίαις πλανώμενοι καὶ ὄρεσιν καὶ σπηλαίοις καὶ ταῖς ὀπαῖς τῆς γῆς. ³⁹ Καὶ οὗτοι πάντες μαρτυρηθέντες διὰ τῆς πίστεως οὐκ ἐκομίσαντο τὴν ἐπαγγελίαν, ⁴⁰ τοῦ θεοῦ περὶ ἡμῶν κρεῖττόν τι προβλεψαμένου, ἵνα μὴ χωρὶς ἡμῶν τελειωθῶσιν.

¹Now faith is the assurance of things hoped for, the conviction of things not seen. ²For by it the men of old received divine approval. ³By faith we understand that the world was created by the word of God, so that what is seen was made out of things which do not appear. ⁴By faith Abel offered to God a more acceptable sacrifice than Cain, through which he received approval as righteous, God bearing witness by accepting his gifts; he died, but through his faith he is still speaking. ⁵By faith Enoch was taken up so that he should not see death; and he was not found, because God had taken him. Now before he was taken he was attested as having pleased God. ⁶And without faith it is impossible to please him. For whoever would draw near to God must believe that he exists and that he rewards those who seek him. ⁷By faith Noah, being warned by God concerning events as yet unseen, took heed and constructed an ark for the saving of his household; by this he condemned the world and became an heir of the righteousness which comes by faith. ⁸By faith Abraham obeyed when he was called to go out to a place which he was to receive as an inheritance; and he went out, not knowing where he was to go. ⁹By faith he sojourned in the land of promise, as in a foreign land, living in tents with Isaac and Jacob, heirs with him of the same promise. ¹⁰For he looked forward to the city which has foundations, whose builder and maker is God. ¹¹By faith Sarah herself received power to conceive, even when she was past the age, since she considered him faithful who had promised. ¹²Therefore from one man, and him as good as dead, were born descendants as many as the stars of heaven and as the innumerable grains of sand by the seashore. ¹³These all died in faith, not having received what was promised, but having seen it and greeted it from afar, and

having acknowledged that they were strangers and exiles on the earth. ¹⁴For people who speak thus make it clear that they are seeking a homeland. ¹⁵If they had been thinking of that land from which they had gone out, they would have had opportunity to return. ¹⁶But as it is, they desire a better country, that is, a heavenly one. Therefore God is not ashamed to be called their God, for he has prepared for them a city. ¹⁷By faith Abraham, when he was tested, offered up Isaac, and he who had received the promises was ready to offer up his only son, ¹⁸of whom it was said, "Through Isaac shall your descendants be named." ¹⁹He considered that God was able to raise men even from the dead; hence, figuratively speaking, he did receive him back. ²⁰By faith Isaac invoked future blessings on Jacob and Esau. ²¹By faith Jacob, when dying, blessed each of the sons of Joseph, bowing in worship over the head of his staff. ²²By faith Joseph, at the end of his life, made mention of the exodus of the Israelites and gave directions concerning his burial.ᵉ ²³By faith Moses, when he was born, was hid for three months by his parents, because they saw that the child was beautiful; and they were not afraid of the king's edict. ²⁴By faith Moses, when he was grown up, refused to be called the son of Pharaoh's daughter, ²⁵choosing rather to share ill-treatment with the people of God than to enjoy the fleeting pleasures of sin. ²⁶He considered abuse suffered for the Christ greater wealth than the treasures of Egypt, for he looked to the reward. ²⁷By faith he left Egypt, not being afraid of the anger of the king; for he endured as seeing him who is invisible. ²⁸By faith he kept the Passover and sprinkled the blood, so that the Destroyer of the first-born might not touch them. ²⁹By faith the people crossed the Red Sea as if on dry land; but the Egyptians, when they attempted to do the same, were drowned. ³⁰By faith the walls of Jericho fell down after they had been encircled for seven days. ³¹By faith Rahab the harlot did not perish with those who were disobedient, because she had *given friendly welcome to the spies.* ³²*And what more shall I say? For time would fail me to tell of Gideon, Barak, Samson, Jephthah, of David and Samuel and the prophets—*³³*who through faith conquered kingdoms, enforced justice, received promises, stopped the mouths of lions,* ³⁴*quenched raging fire, escaped the edge of the sword, won strength out of weakness, became mighty in war, put foreign armies to flight.* ³⁵*Women received their dead by resurrection. Some were tortured, refusing to accept release, that they might rise again to a better life.* ³⁶*Others suffered mocking and scourging, and even chains and imprisonment.* ³⁷*They were stoned, they were sawn in two,*ᵉ *they were killed with the sword; they went about in skins of sheep and goats, destitute, afflicted, ill-treated—*³⁸*of whom the world was not worthy—wandering over deserts and mountains, and in dens and caves of the earth.* ³⁹*And all these, though well attested by their faith, did not receive what was promised,* ⁴⁰*since God had foreseen something better for us, that apart from us they should not be made perfect.*

Since the end of the road lies far ahead and cannot even be seen by the hearers, the author invites them to understand that they can only hope to reach it. And such hope requires continual trust (*pistis*; faith) with full conviction that the divine promise will be realized so long as they keep proceeding on the "way" required by the Law, whether written on tablets or on hearts. In order to underscore this reality, he provides examples of such trust through a long list of their predecessors who lived under the Mosaic law, and even before that, the like of Abel, Enoch, Noah, Abraham, Sarah, and Joseph, while relegating examples of their contemporaries until much later (13:7). In other words, the models he offers his hearers have already been "scripturalized," that is, "attested" (*martyrēthentes*; witnessed to [11:39]) by God himself and thus are irrefutable.

The teaching of keeping hope alive through trust in the Lord's promise is thoroughly Pauline. The quintessential expression of this trust is to persevere in brotherly love (13:1), in spite of any afflictions associated with doing so:

> For through the Spirit, by faith, we wait for the hope of righteousness. For in Christ Jesus neither circumcision nor uncircumcision is of any avail, but faith working through love. (Gal 5:5-6)

> Therefore, since we are justified by faith, we have peace with God through our Lord Jesus Christ. Through him we have obtained access to this grace in which we stand, and we rejoice in our hope of sharing the glory of God. More than that, we rejoice in our sufferings, knowing that suffering produces endurance, and endurance produces character, and character produces hope, and hope does not disappoint us, because God's love has been poured into our hearts through the Holy Spirit which has been given to us. (Rom 5:1-5)

> For in this hope we were saved. Now hope that is seen is not hope. For who hopes for what he sees? But if we hope for what we do not see, we wait for it with patience. (Rom 8:24-25)

> Blessed be the God and Father of our Lord Jesus Christ, the Father of mercies and God of all comfort, who comforts us in all our affliction, so that we may be able to comfort those who are in any affliction, with the comfort with which we ourselves are comforted by God. For as we share abundantly in Christ's sufferings, so through Christ we share abundantly in comfort too. If we are afflicted, it is for your comfort and salvation; and if we are comforted, it is for your comfort, which you experience when you patiently endure the same sufferings that we suffer. Our hope for you is unshaken; for we know that as you share in our sufferings, you will also share in our comfort. (2 Cor 1:3-7)

For this reason, because I have heard of your faith in the Lord Jesus and your love toward all the saints, I do not cease to give thanks for you, remembering you in my prayers, that the God of our Lord Jesus Christ, the Father of glory, may give you a spirit of wisdom and of revelation in the knowledge of him, having the eyes of your hearts enlightened, that you may know what is the hope to which he has called you, what are the riches of his glorious inheritance in the saints, and what is the immeasurable greatness of his power in us who believe. (Eph 1:15-19a)

We always thank God, the Father of our Lord Jesus Christ, when we pray for you, because we have heard of your faith in Christ Jesus and of the love which you have for all the saints, because of the hope laid up for you in heaven. (Col 1:3-5a)

We give thanks to God always for you all, constantly mentioning you in our prayers, remembering before our God and Father your work of faith and labor of love and steadfastness of hope in our Lord Jesus Christ. For we know, brethren beloved by God, that he has chosen you; for our gospel came to you not only in word, but also in power and in the Holy Spirit and with full conviction. You know what kind of men we proved to be among you for your sake. And you became imitators of us and of the Lord, for you received the word in much affliction, with joy inspired by the Holy Spirit; so that you became an example to all the believers in Macedonia and in Achaia. (1 Thess 1:2-7)

We are bound to give thanks to God always for you, brethren, as is fitting, because your faith is growing abundantly, and the love of every one of you for one another is increasing. Therefore we ourselves boast of you in the churches of God for your steadfastness and faith in all your persecutions and in the afflictions which you are enduring. This is evidence of the righteous judgment of God, that you may be made worthy of the kingdom of God, for which you are suffering—since indeed God deems it just to repay with affliction those who afflict you, and to grant rest with us to you who are afflicted, when the Lord Jesus is revealed from heaven with his mighty angels in flaming fire. (2 Thess 1:3-7)

The underlying common denominator for the scriptural models cited in Hebrews 11 is the abiding trust the witnesses (12:1) exhibited in spite of adversities, which sometimes were humanly unbearable. Of import is the total cumulative effect rather than the details of each and every example. It is the cadence of the eighteen "by faith" that holds the entire chapter together. Yet even the eighteen examples are not exhaustive: "And what more shall I say? For time would fail me to tell of Gideon, Barak, Samson, Jephthah, of David and Samuel and the prophets" (11:32). This is followed by an editorialized general description of afflictions that hit home with the hearers themselves, similar to what we have in Romans and in the Corinthian correspondence:

> ... who through faith conquered kingdoms, enforced justice, received promises, stopped the mouths of lions, quenched raging fire, escaped the edge of the sword, won strength out of weakness, became mighty in war, put foreign armies to flight. Women received their dead by resurrection. Some were tortured, refusing to accept release, that they might rise again to a better life. Others suffered mocking and scourging, and even chains and imprisonment. They were stoned, they were sawn in two, they were killed with the sword; they went about in skins of sheep and goats, destitute, afflicted, ill-treated—of whom the world was not worthy—wandering over deserts and mountains, and in dens and caves of the earth. (Heb 11:33-38)

Who shall separate us from the love of Christ? Shall tribulation, or distress, or persecution, or famine, or nakedness, or peril, or sword? As it is written, "For thy sake we are being killed all the day long; we are regarded as sheep to be slaughtered." (Rom 8:35-36)

For I think that God has exhibited us apostles as last of all, like men sentenced to death; because we have become a spectacle to the world, to angels and to men. We are fools for Christ's sake, but you are wise in Christ. We are weak, but you are strong. You are held in honor, but we in disrepute. To the present hour we hunger and thirst, we are ill-clad and buffeted and homeless, and we labor, working with our own hands. When reviled, we bless; when persecuted, we endure; when slandered, we try to conciliate; we have become, and are now, as the refuse of the world, the offscouring of all things. (1 Cor 4:9-13)

But we have this treasure in earthen vessels, to show that the transcendent power belongs to God and not to us. We are afflicted in every way, but not crushed; perplexed, but not driven to despair; persecuted, but not forsaken; struck down, but not destroyed; always carrying in the body the death of Jesus, so that the life of Jesus may also be manifested in our bodies. For while we live we are always being given up to death for Jesus' sake, so that the life of Jesus may be manifested in our mortal flesh. So death is at work in us, but life in you. (2 Cor 4:7-12)

Are they servants of Christ? I am a better one—I am talking like a madman—with far greater labors, far more imprisonments, with countless beatings, and often near death. Five times I have received at the hands of the Jews the forty lashes less one. Three times I have been beaten with rods; once I was stoned. Three times I have been shipwrecked; a night and a day I have been adrift at sea; on frequent journeys, in danger from rivers, danger from robbers, danger from my own people, danger from Gentiles, danger in the city, danger in the wilderness, danger at sea, danger from false brethren; in toil and hardship, through many a sleepless night, in hunger and thirst, often without food, in cold and exposure. And, apart from other things, there is the daily pressure upon me of my anxiety for all the churches. Who is weak, and I am not weak? Who is made to fall, and I am not indignant? (11:23-29)

Still, the real twist comes with the conclusion: "And all these, though well attested (*martyrēthentes*) by their faith, *did not receive* what was promised (*tēn epangelian*; the promise), since God had foreseen something better for us, that apart from us they should not be made perfect (*teleiōthēsan*)." (Heb 11:39-40) So the full realization of the one promise to all will take place at the end when the nations, together with Israel, will share the promised life in "Mount Zion ... the city of the living God, the heavenly Jerusalem" (12:22), as Isaiah foretold:

> I am coming to gather all nations and tongues; and they shall come and shall see my glory, and I will set a sign among them. And from them I will send survivors to the nations, to Tarshish, Put, and Lud, who draw the bow, to Tubal and Javan, to the coastlands afar off, that have not heard my fame or seen my glory; and they shall declare my glory among the nations. And they shall bring all your brethren from all the nations as an offering to the Lord, upon horses, and in chariots, and in litters, and upon mules, and upon dromedaries, to my holy mountain Jerusalem, says the Lord, just as the Israelites bring their cereal offering in a clean vessel to the house of the Lord. And some of them also I will take for priests and for Levites, says the Lord. (66:18b-21)

By the same token, if the "men of old" (*presbyteroi*; elders [Heb 11:2) had to wait for "us" (v.40), we, in turn, will have to patiently wait for those who will come after "us."

Chapter 12

Vv. 12:1-29 ¹Τοιγαροῦν καὶ ἡμεῖς τοσοῦτον ἔχοντες περικείμενον ἡμῖν νέφος μαρτύρων, ὄγκον ἀποθέμενοι πάντα καὶ τὴν εὐπερίστατον ἁμαρτίαν, δι᾽ ὑπομονῆς τρέχωμεν τὸν προκείμενον ἡμῖν ἀγῶνα ²ἀφορῶντες εἰς τὸν τῆς πίστεως ἀρχηγὸν καὶ τελειωτὴν Ἰησοῦν, ὃς ἀντὶ τῆς προκειμένης αὐτῷ χαρᾶς ὑπέμεινεν σταυρὸν αἰσχύνης καταφρονήσας ἐν δεξιᾷ τε τοῦ θρόνου τοῦ θεοῦ κεκάθικεν. ³ἀναλογίσασθε γὰρ τὸν τοιαύτην ὑπομεμενηκότα ὑπὸ τῶν ἁμαρτωλῶν εἰς ἑαυτὸν ἀντιλογίαν, ἵνα μὴ κάμητε ταῖς ψυχαῖς ὑμῶν ἐκλυόμενοι. ⁴Οὔπω μέχρις αἵματος ἀντικατέστητε πρὸς τὴν ἁμαρτίαν ἀνταγωνιζόμενοι. ⁵καὶ ἐκλέλησθε τῆς παρακλήσεως, ἥτις ὑμῖν ὡς υἱοῖς διαλέγεται· υἱέ μου, μὴ ὀλιγώρει παιδείας κυρίου μηδὲ ἐκλύου ὑπ᾽ αὐτοῦ ἐλεγχόμενος· ⁶ὃν γὰρ ἀγαπᾷ κύριος παιδεύει, μαστιγοῖ δὲ πάντα υἱὸν ὃν παραδέχεται. ⁷εἰς παιδείαν ὑπομένετε, ὡς υἱοῖς ὑμῖν προσφέρεται ὁ θεός. τίς γὰρ υἱὸς ὃν οὐ παιδεύει πατήρ; ⁸εἰ δὲ χωρίς ἐστε παιδείας ἧς μέτοχοι γεγόνασιν πάντες, ἄρα νόθοι καὶ οὐχ υἱοί ἐστε. ⁹εἶτα τοὺς μὲν τῆς σαρκὸς ἡμῶν πατέρας εἴχομεν παιδευτὰς καὶ ἐνετρεπόμεθα· οὐ πολὺ [δὲ] μᾶλλον ὑποταγησόμεθα τῷ πατρὶ τῶν πνευμάτων καὶ ζήσομεν; ¹⁰οἱ μὲν γὰρ πρὸς ὀλίγας ἡμέρας κατὰ τὸ δοκοῦν αὐτοῖς ἐπαίδευον, ὁ δὲ ἐπὶ τὸ συμφέρον εἰς τὸ μεταλαβεῖν τῆς ἁγιότητος αὐτοῦ. ¹¹πᾶσα δὲ παιδεία πρὸς μὲν τὸ παρὸν οὐ δοκεῖ χαρᾶς εἶναι ἀλλὰ λύπης, ὕστερον δὲ καρπὸν εἰρηνικὸν τοῖς δι᾽ αὐτῆς γεγυμνασμένοις ἀποδίδωσιν δικαιοσύνης. ¹²Διὸ τὰς παρειμένας χεῖρας καὶ τὰ παραλελυμένα γόνατα ἀνορθώσατε, ¹³καὶ τροχιὰς ὀρθὰς ποιεῖτε τοῖς ποσὶν ὑμῶν, ἵνα μὴ τὸ χωλὸν ἐκτραπῇ, ἰαθῇ δὲ μᾶλλον. ¹⁴Εἰρήνην διώκετε μετὰ πάντων καὶ τὸν ἁγιασμόν, οὗ χωρὶς οὐδεὶς ὄψεται τὸν κύριον, ¹⁵ἐπισκοποῦντες μή τις ὑστερῶν ἀπὸ τῆς χάριτος τοῦ θεοῦ, μή τις ῥίζα πικρίας ἄνω φύουσα ἐνοχλῇ καὶ δι᾽ αὐτῆς μιανθῶσιν πολλοί, ¹⁶μή τις πόρνος ἢ βέβηλος ὡς Ἠσαῦ, ὃς ἀντὶ βρώσεως μιᾶς ἀπέδετο τὰ πρωτοτόκια ἑαυτοῦ. ¹⁷ἴστε γὰρ ὅτι καὶ μετέπειτα θέλων κληρονομῆσαι τὴν εὐλογίαν ἀπεδοκιμάσθη, μετανοίας γὰρ τόπον οὐχ εὗρεν καίπερ μετὰ δακρύων ἐκζητήσας αὐτήν. ¹⁸Οὐ γὰρ προσεληλύθατε ψηλαφωμένῳ καὶ κεκαυμένῳ πυρὶ καὶ γνόφῳ καὶ ζόφῳ καὶ θυέλλῃ ¹⁹καὶ σάλπιγγος ἤχῳ καὶ φωνῇ ῥημάτων, ἧς οἱ ἀκούσαντες παρῃτήσαντο μὴ προστεθῆναι αὐτοῖς λόγον, ²⁰οὐκ ἔφερον γὰρ τὸ διαστελλόμενον· κἂν θηρίον θίγῃ τοῦ ὄρους, λιθοβοληθήσεται· ²¹καί, οὕτω φοβερὸν ἦν τὸ φανταζόμενον, Μωϋσῆς εἶπεν· ἔκφοβός εἰμι καὶ ἔντρομος. ²²ἀλλὰ προσεληλύθατε Σιὼν ὄρει καὶ πόλει θεοῦ ζῶντος, Ἰερουσαλὴμ ἐπουρανίῳ, καὶ μυριάσιν ἀγγέλων, πανηγύρει ²³καὶ ἐκκλησίᾳ πρωτοτόκων ἀπογεγραμμένων ἐν οὐρανοῖς καὶ κριτῇ θεῷ πάντων καὶ πνεύμασι δικαίων τετελειωμένων ²⁴καὶ διαθήκης νέας μεσίτῃ Ἰησοῦ καὶ αἵματι ῥαντισμοῦ κρεῖττον λαλοῦντι παρὰ τὸν Ἅβελ. ²⁵Βλέπετε μὴ παραιτήσησθε τὸν λαλοῦντα· εἰ γὰρ ἐκεῖνοι οὐκ ἐξέφυγον ἐπὶ γῆς παραιτησάμενοι τὸν χρηματίζοντα, πολὺ μᾶλλον ἡμεῖς οἱ τὸν ἀπ' οὐρανῶν ἀποστρεφόμενοι, ²⁶οὗ ἡ φωνὴ τὴν γῆν ἐσάλευσεν τότε, νῦν δὲ ἐπήγγελται λέγων· ἔτι ἅπαξ ἐγὼ σείσω οὐ μόνον τὴν γῆν ἀλλὰ καὶ τὸν οὐρανόν. ²⁷τὸ δὲ ἔτι ἅπαξ δηλοῖ [τὴν] τῶν σαλευομένων μετάθεσιν ὡς πεποιημένων, ἵνα μείνῃ τὰ μὴ σαλευόμενα. ²⁸Διὸ βασιλείαν ἀσάλευτον παραλαμβάνοντες ἔχωμεν χάριν, δι' ἧς λατρεύωμεν εὐαρέστως τῷ θεῷ μετὰ εὐλαβείας καὶ δέους· ²⁹καὶ γὰρ ὁ θεὸς ἡμῶν πῦρ καταναλίσκον.

¹Therefore, since we are surrounded by so great a cloud of witnesses, let us also lay aside every weight, and sin which clings so closely, and let us run with perseverance the race that is set before us, ²looking to Jesus the pioneer and perfecter of our faith, who for the joy that was set before him endured the cross, despising the shame, and is seated at the right hand of the throne of God. ³Consider him who endured from sinners such hostility against himself, so that you may not grow weary or fainthearted. ⁴In your struggle against sin you have not yet resisted to the point of shedding your blood. ⁵And have you forgotten the exhortation which addresses you as sons?—"My son, do not regard lightly the discipline of the Lord, nor lose courage when you are punished by him. ⁶For the Lord disciplines him whom he loves, and chastises every son whom he receives." ⁷It is for discipline that you have to endure. God is treating you as sons; for what son is there whom his father does not discipline? ⁸If you are left without discipline, in which all have participated, then you are illegitimate children and not sons. ⁹Besides this, we have had earthly fathers to discipline us and we respected them. Shall we not much more be subject to the Father of spirits and live? ¹⁰For they disciplined us for a short time at their pleasure, but he disciplines us for our good, that we may share his holiness. ¹¹For the moment all discipline seems painful rather than pleasant; later it yields the peaceful fruit of righteousness to those who have been trained by it. ¹²Therefore lift your drooping hands and strengthen your weak knees, ¹³and make straight paths for your feet, so that what is lame may not be put out of joint but rather be healed.

¹⁴Strive for peace with all men, and for the holiness without which no one will see the Lord.¹⁵See to it that no one fail to obtain the grace of God; that no "root of bitterness" spring up and cause trouble, and by it the many become defiled; ¹⁶that no one be immoral or irreligious like Esau, who sold his birthright for a single meal. ¹⁷For you know that afterward, when he desired to inherit the blessing, he was rejected, for he found no chance to repent, though he sought it with tears. ¹⁸For you have not come to what may be touched, a blazing fire, and darkness, and gloom, and a tempest, ¹⁹and the sound of a trumpet, and a voice whose words made the hearers entreat that no further messages be spoken to them. ²⁰For they could not endure the order that was given, "If even a beast touches the mountain, it shall be stoned." ²¹Indeed, so terrifying was the sight that Moses said, "I tremble with fear." ²²But you have come to Mount Zion and to the city of the living God, the heavenly Jerusalem, and to innumerable angels in festal gathering, ²³and to the assembly of the first-born who are enrolled in heaven, and to a judge who is God of all, and to the spirits of just men made perfect, ²⁴and to Jesus, the mediator of a new covenant, and to the sprinkled

blood that speaks more graciously than the blood of Abel. ²⁵*See that you do not refuse him who is speaking. For if they did not escape when they refused him who warned them on earth, much less shall we escape if we reject him who warns from heaven.* ²⁶*His voice then shook the earth; but now he has promised, "Yet once more I will shake not only the earth but also the heaven."* ²⁷*This phrase, "Yet once more," indicates the removal of what is shaken, as of what has been made, in order that what cannot be shaken may remain.* ²⁸*Therefore let us be grateful for receiving a kingdom that cannot be shaken, and thus let us offer to God acceptable worship, with reverence and awe;* ²⁹*for our God is a consuming fire.*

Chapter 11 is a lengthy aside that urges the hearers to maintain their hope. After that exhortation, the author picks up in chapter 12 where he left off at the end of chapter 10:

> But recall the former days when, after you were enlightened, you endured (*hypomeinate*) a hard struggle with sufferings ... For you have need of endurance (*hypomonēs*), so that you may do the will of God and receive what is promised. (10:32, 36)

> *Therefore*, since we are surrounded by so great a cloud of witnesses, let us also lay aside every weight, and sin which clings so closely, and let us run with perseverance (*hypomonēs*) the race that is set before us, looking to Jesus the pioneer (*arkhēgon*) and perfecter (*teleiōtēn*) of our faith, who for the joy that was set before him endured (*hypemeinen*) the cross, despising the shame, and is seated at the right hand of the throne of God. Consider him who endured (*hypomemenēkota*) from sinners such hostility against himself, so that you may not grow weary or fainthearted ... It is for discipline that you have to endure (*hypomenete*). (12:1-3, 7)

The only instances of the root *hypomen*— in Hebrews occur in these verses. *hypomonēs* is the other facet of hope.[1] That is to say, in spite of the assurance of hope, one must persevere until one "receives the promise." To stress this, Paul used the metaphor of "running the race."[2] In other words, the "end" never comes before the race has been run and has ended—the end in scripture being either at the Lord's coming or at one's death: "For I am already on the point of being sacrificed; the time of my departure has come. I have fought the good fight, I have finished the race, I have kept the faith." (2 Tim 4:6-7) This quintessential Pauline teaching overarches the entire movement of Hebrews and, for all practical purposes, is at the heart of the writer's "exhortation" (*paraklēsis*).

Early on the hearers are instructed to follow the lead of Jesus, who is described in these terms:

> For it was fitting that he, for whom and by whom all things exist, in bringing many sons to glory, should make the pioneer (*arkhēgon*) of their salvation perfect (*teleiōsai*) through *suffering*. For he who sanctifies and those who are sanctified have all one origin. That is why he is not ashamed (*epeskhynetai*) to call them brethren, saying, "I will proclaim thy name to my brethren, in the midst of the congregation I will praise thee." And again, "I will put my trust in him." And again, "Here am I, and the children God has given me" … Christ was faithful over God's house as a son. And we are his house if we hold fast our confidence and pride in our *hope* … But exhort (*parakaleite*) one another every day, as long as it is called "today," that none of you may be hardened by the deceitfulness of sin. (Heb 2:10-13; 3:6, 13)

---

[1] See *1 Thess* 39-40.
[2] 1 Cor 9:24, 26; Gal 2:2; 5:7; Phil 2:16; 2 Tim 4:7.

Mid-way through the letter one hears:

> So when God desired to show more convincingly to the heirs of the *promise* the unchangeable character of his purpose, he interposed with an oath, so that through two unchangeable things, in which it is impossible that God should prove false, we who have fled for refuge might have strong encouragement (*paraklēsin*) to seize the *hope* set before us. We have this as a sure and steadfast anchor of the soul, a hope that enters into the inner shrine behind the curtain, where Jesus has gone as a *forerunner* on our behalf, having become a high priest for ever after the order of Melchizedek. (6:17-20)

Toward the end of the letter we have a forceful and encompassing recapitulation:

> Let us hold fast the confession of our *hope* without wavering, for he who promised is faithful (*pistos*) and let us consider how to stir up one another to love and good works, not neglecting to meet together, as is the habit of some, but encouraging (*parakalountes*) one another, and all the more as you see the Day drawing near ... But recall the former days when, after you were enlightened, you endured (*hypomeinate*) a hard struggle with *sufferings* ... For you have need of endurance (*hypomonēs*), so that you may do the will of God and receive *what is promised*. (10: 23-25, 32, 36)

> Therefore, since we are surrounded by so great a cloud of witnesses, let us also lay aside every weight, and sin which clings so closely, and let us run with perseverance (*hypomonēs*) the race that is set before us, looking to Jesus the pioneer (*arkhēgon*) and perfecter (*teleiōtēn*) of our faith, who for the joy that was set before him endured (*hypemeinen*) the cross, despising the shame, and is seated at the right hand of the throne of God. Consider him who endured (*hypomemenēkota*) from sinners such hostility against himself, so that you may not grow weary or fainthearted ... It is for discipline that you have to endure (*hypomenete*) ... (12:1-3, 7)

Finally, at the conclusion of the letter the author pleads:

> "I appeal (*parakalō*) to you, brethren, bear with my word of exhortation (*paraklēseōs*), for I have written to you briefly." (13:22)

So the new covenant does not entail a lack of judgment on God's part. To the contrary, compared with the old covenant, the regimen under the new one is by far more ominous, precisely because the grace is greater and more encompassing (12:18-24). That is why the author saved the "negative" example of Esau selling his birthright for a single meal until the end: "For you know that afterward, when he [Esau] desired to inherit the blessing, he was rejected, for he found no chance to repent, though he sought it with tears." (v.17) Hence his lengthy caveat that the hearers not act similarly (vv.25-28). It is, after all, *because* "our God is a consuming fire" (v.29)[3] that he disciplines us as a father would his children (vv.5-6), a discipline "that you have to endure [with patience] (*hypomenete*)" (v.7a). And the reasoning behind this is as evident as it is simple:

> God is treating you as sons; for *what son is there whom his father does not discipline*? If you are left without discipline, in which all have participated, *then you are illegitimate children and not sons*. Besides this, we have had earthly fathers to discipline us and we respected them. *Shall we not much more be subject to the Father of spirits and live*? For they disciplined us for a short time at their pleasure, but *he disciplines us for our good*, that we may share his holiness. *For the moment all discipline seems painful rather than pleasant; later it yields the peaceful fruit of righteousness to those who have been trained by it.* (vv.7-11)

---

[3] The importance of this thought can be seen in that it was referred to earlier: "For if we sin deliberately after receiving the knowledge of the truth, there no longer remains a sacrifice for sins, but a fearful prospect of judgment, and a fury of fire which will consume the adversaries." (10:26-27)

Chapter 13

Vv. 13:1-25 ¹Ἡ φιλαδελφία μενέτω. ²τῆς φιλοξενίας μὴ ἐπιλανθάνεσθε, διὰ ταύτης γὰρ ἔλαθόν τινες ξενίσαντες ἀγγέλους. ³μιμνήσκεσθε τῶν δεσμίων ὡς συνδεδεμένοι, τῶν κακουχουμένων ὡς καὶ αὐτοὶ ὄντες ἐν σώματι. ⁴Τίμιος ὁ γάμος ἐν πᾶσιν καὶ ἡ κοίτη ἀμίαντος, πόρνους γὰρ καὶ μοιχοὺς κρινεῖ ὁ θεός. ⁵Ἀφιλάργυρος ὁ τρόπος, ἀρκούμενοι τοῖς παροῦσιν. αὐτὸς γὰρ εἴρηκεν· οὐ μή σε ἀνῶ οὐδ᾽ οὐ μή σε ἐγκαταλίπω, ⁶ὥστε θαρροῦντας ἡμᾶς λέγειν· κύριος ἐμοὶ βοηθός, [καὶ] οὐ φοβηθήσομαι, τί ποιήσει μοι ἄνθρωπος; ⁷Μνημονεύετε τῶν ἡγουμένων ὑμῶν, οἵτινες ἐλάλησαν ὑμῖν τὸν λόγον τοῦ θεοῦ, ὧν ἀναθεωροῦντες τὴν ἔκβασιν τῆς ἀναστροφῆς μιμεῖσθε τὴν πίστιν. ⁸Ἰησοῦς Χριστὸς ἐχθὲς καὶ σήμερον ὁ αὐτὸς καὶ εἰς τοὺς αἰῶνας. ⁹Διδαχαῖς ποικίλαις καὶ ξέναις μὴ παραφέρεσθε· καλὸν γὰρ χάριτι βεβαιοῦσθαι τὴν καρδίαν, οὐ βρώμασιν ἐν οἷς οὐκ ὠφελήθησαν οἱ περιπατοῦντες. ¹⁰ἔχομεν θυσιαστήριον ἐξ οὗ φαγεῖν οὐκ ἔχουσιν ἐξουσίαν οἱ τῇ σκηνῇ λατρεύοντες. ¹¹ὧν γὰρ εἰσφέρεται ζώων τὸ αἷμα περὶ ἁμαρτίας εἰς τὰ ἅγια διὰ τοῦ ἀρχιερέως, τούτων τὰ σώματα κατακαίεται ἔξω τῆς παρεμβολῆς. ¹²Διὸ καὶ Ἰησοῦς, ἵνα ἁγιάσῃ διὰ τοῦ ἰδίου αἵματος τὸν λαόν, ἔξω τῆς πύλης ἔπαθεν. ¹³τοίνυν ἐξερχώμεθα πρὸς αὐτὸν ἔξω τῆς παρεμβολῆς τὸν ὀνειδισμὸν αὐτοῦ φέροντες· ¹⁴οὐ γὰρ ἔχομεν ὧδε μένουσαν πόλιν ἀλλὰ τὴν μέλλουσαν ἐπιζητοῦμεν. ¹⁵Δι᾽ αὐτοῦ [οὖν] ἀναφέρωμεν θυσίαν αἰνέσεως διὰ παντὸς τῷ θεῷ, τοῦτ᾽ ἔστιν καρπὸν χειλέων ὁμολογούντων τῷ ὀνόματι αὐτοῦ. ¹⁶τῆς δὲ εὐποιΐας καὶ κοινωνίας μὴ ἐπιλανθάνεσθε· τοιαύταις γὰρ θυσίαις εὐαρεστεῖται ὁ θεός. ¹⁷Πείθεσθε τοῖς ἡγουμένοις ὑμῶν καὶ ὑπείκετε, αὐτοὶ γὰρ ἀγρυπνοῦσιν ὑπὲρ τῶν ψυχῶν ὑμῶν ὡς λόγον ἀποδώσοντες, ἵνα μετὰ χαρᾶς τοῦτο ποιῶσιν καὶ μὴ στενάζοντες· ἀλυσιτελὲς γὰρ ὑμῖν τοῦτο. ¹⁸Προσεύχεσθε περὶ ἡμῶν· πειθόμεθα γὰρ ὅτι καλὴν συνείδησιν ἔχομεν, ἐν πᾶσιν καλῶς θέλοντες ἀναστρέφεσθαι. ¹⁹περισσοτέρως δὲ παρακαλῶ τοῦτο ποιῆσαι, ἵνα τάχιον ἀποκατασταθῶ ὑμῖν. ²⁰ Ὁ δὲ θεὸς τῆς εἰρήνης, ὁ ἀναγαγὼν ἐκ νεκρῶν τὸν ποιμένα τῶν προβάτων τὸν μέγαν ἐν αἵματι διαθήκης αἰωνίου, τὸν κύριον ἡμῶν Ἰησοῦν, ²¹καταρτίσαι ὑμᾶς ἐν παντὶ ἀγαθῷ εἰς τὸ ποιῆσαι τὸ θέλημα αὐτοῦ, ποιῶν ἐν ἡμῖν τὸ εὐάρεστον ἐνώπιον αὐτοῦ διὰ Ἰησοῦ

Χριστοῦ, ᾧ ἡ δόξα εἰς τοὺς αἰῶνας [τῶν αἰώνων], ἀμήν. ²²Παρακαλῶ δὲ ὑμᾶς, ἀδελφοί, ἀνέχεσθε τοῦ λόγου τῆς παρακλήσεως, καὶ γὰρ διὰ βραχέων ἐπέστειλα ὑμῖν. ²³Γινώσκετε τὸν ἀδελφὸν ἡμῶν Τιμόθεον ἀπολελυμένον, μεθ᾽ οὗ ἐὰν τάχιον ἔρχηται ὄψομαι ὑμᾶς. ²⁴Ἀσπάσασθε πάντας τοὺς ἡγουμένους ὑμῶν καὶ πάντας τοὺς ἁγίους. Ἀσπάζονται ὑμᾶς οἱ ἀπὸ τῆς Ἰταλίας. ²⁵Ἡ χάρις μετὰ πάντων ὑμῶν.

¹*Let brotherly love continue.* ²*Do not neglect to show hospitality to strangers, for thereby some have entertained angels unawares.* ³*Remember those who are in prison, as though in prison with them; and those who are ill-treated, since you also are in the body.* ⁴*Let marriage be held in honor among all, and let the marriage bed be undefiled; for God will judge the immoral and adulterous.* ⁵*Keep your life free from love of money, and be content with what you have; for he has said, "I will never fail you nor forsake you."* ⁶*Hence we can confidently say, "The Lord is my helper, I will not be afraid; what can man do to me?"* ⁷*Remember your leaders, those who spoke to you the word of God; consider the outcome of their life, and imitate their faith.* ⁸*Jesus Christ is the same yesterday and today and for ever.* ⁹*Do not be led away by diverse and strange teachings; for it is well that the heart be strengthened by grace, not by foods, which have not benefited their adherents.* ¹⁰*We have an altar from which those who serve the tent have no right to eat.* ¹¹*For the bodies of those animals whose blood is brought into the sanctuary by the high priest as a sacrifice for sin are burned outside the camp.* ¹²*So Jesus also suffered outside the gate in order to sanctify the people through his own blood.* ¹³*Therefore let us go forth to him outside the camp and bear the abuse he endured.* ¹⁴*For here we have no lasting city, but we seek the city which is to come.* ¹⁵*Through him then let us continually offer up a sacrifice of praise to God, that is, the fruit of lips that acknowledge his name.* ¹⁶*Do not neglect to do good and to share what you have,*

for such sacrifices are pleasing to God. ¹⁷*Obey your leaders and submit to them; for they are keeping watch over your souls, as men who will have to give account. Let them do this joyfully, and not sadly, for that would be of no advantage to you.* ¹⁸*Pray for us, for we are sure that we have a clear conscience, desiring to act honorably in all things.* ¹⁹*I urge you the more earnestly to do this in order that I may be restored to you the sooner.* ²⁰*Now may the God of peace who brought again from the dead our Lord Jesus, the great shepherd of the sheep, by the blood of the eternal covenant,* ²¹*equip you with everything good that you may do his will, working in you that which is pleasing in his sight, through Jesus Christ; to whom be glory for ever and ever. Amen.* ²²*I appeal to you, brethren, bear with my word of exhortation, for I have written to you briefly.* ²³*You should understand that our brother Timothy has been released, with whom I shall see you if he comes soon.* ²⁴*Greet all your leaders and all the saints. Those who come from Italy send you greetings.* ²⁵*Grace be with all of you. Amen.*

Now that he is nearing the end of his letter, the author reminds his hearers of the heart of the Pauline gospel: the love for the needy neighbor. He begins by referring to it twice, using the classical terms of love and hospitality:

> Let *brotherly love* (*philadelphia*)¹ continue. Do not neglect to show *hospitality to strangers* (*philoxenias*),² for some have entertained angels unawares. Remember those who are in prison, as though in prison with them; and those who are ill-treated, since you also are in the body. (13:1-3)

---

¹ Rom 12:10; 1 Thess 4:9.
² Rom 12:13. The fact that *philadelphia* and *philoxenia* are mentioned back to back in this order in both Romans and Hebrews, militates for the parallelism between those letters (see further on this matter in *NTI₄* 80-83).

He even revisits this matter twice more—in the middle and at the end of the chapter:

> Do not neglect to do good and to share what you have, for such sacrifices are pleasing to God. (v.16)

> Now may the God of peace who brought again from the dead our Lord Jesus, the great shepherd of the sheep, by the blood of the eternal covenant, equip you with everything good that you may do his will, working in you that which is pleasing in his sight, through Jesus Christ; to whom be glory for ever and ever. Amen. (vv.20-21)

This topic is not simply an afterthought. The author prepared for it in the previous chapters:

> But recall the former days when, after you were enlightened, you endured a hard struggle with sufferings, sometimes being publicly exposed to abuse and affliction, and sometimes being partners with those so treated. For you had compassion on the prisoners, and you joyfully accepted the plundering of your property, since you knew that you yourselves had a better possession and an abiding one. (10:32-34)[3]

> Strive for peace with all men,[4] and for the holiness without which no one will see the Lord. (12:14)

Another oblique indication that the love for the needy neighbor is the fulfillment of the Law and by extension of the entire Old Testament scripture[5] can be found in the concluding

---

[3] Notice the closeness in terminology as well as thought: in both cases, one hears of prisoners and those ill-treated, on whom the hearers are asked to have compassion as having themselves undergone similar experiences.
[4] Notice the correspondence with 13:20 where reference is made to the "God of peace."
[5] Paul taught this at two occasions (Gal 5:13-15; Rom 13:8-10).

verses of the passage dealing with this topic. The divine statement "I will never fail you nor forsake you" (Heb 13:5) is taken from Deuteronomy (31:6), the last book of the Law, thus giving the impression that God will be on the side of those who fulfill his law through their care for the needy neighbor. What is equally if not more impressive is that "our" response to that is cast in words taken from Psalm 118:6: "The Lord is my helper, I will not be afraid; what can man do to me?" Since the main concern of Hebrews is the liturgical service in the "tent" of the new Zion, most of the scriptural quotations are taken from the Book of Psalms. Specific passages from Psalm 2 and 110 bracket the entire book. When one takes into consideration that the Book of Psalms is divided in five "parts" or "books" (1-41; 42-72; 73-89; 90-106; 107-150)—a division obviously intended to mimic the five books of the Law—then the clear impression is that the author is covering all five parts of Psalms. By opting to choose "our" response from a psalm beyond Psalm 110, the author is indirectly forcing out of the hearers an "Amen" to his teaching about the Book of Psalms in this letter and more specifically to Hebrews 13:1-4 and, by the same token, an "Amen" to his "exhortation" that his hearers continue on this path.

Having reminded his hearers of the core of the gospel message, all that remains is for the author to leave his "exhortation," imbedded in this letter, as a legacy to them: "I appeal (*Parakalō*) to you, brethren, bear with my word (*logos*; apostolic message) of exhortation (*paraklēseōs*), for I have written (*epesteila*; have written as an epistle [*epistolē*]) to you briefly." (13:22) This ingeniously construed verse in the original concludes this "brief" letter that opened with reference to the apostolic message being an invitation to full table fellowship between all human beings, Jews and Gentiles alike, which is the condition for the ultimate salvation wrought by God through his Christ: "Are they not all ministering spirits sent forth (*apostellomena*; from the verb *apostello* whence *apostolos* [apostle]) to serve, for the sake of those who are to obtain (*klēronomein*; inherit) salvation?" (1:14); "Therefore, holy brethren, who share in a heavenly call (*klēseōs*; from the same root as *paraklēseōs*), consider Jesus, the *apostle* (*apostolon*) and high priest of our confession." (3:1) The intended link between these statements is evident in the fact that they contain the only three terms from the verb *stellō* (prepare to go; equip to send out) in this letter. In other words, the author is committing to a writ his teaching for all upcoming generations of hearers, which is a lesson Paul learned from the Old Testament prophets and bequeathed to his school that authored the New Testament:

> Then Jeremiah called Baruch the son of Neriah, and Baruch wrote upon a scroll at the dictation of Jeremiah all the words of the Lord which he had spoken to him. And Jeremiah ordered Baruch, saying, "I am debarred from going to the house of the Lord; so you are to go, and on a fast day in the hearing of all the people in the Lord's house you shall read the words of the Lord from the scroll which you have written at my dictation. You shall read them also in the hearing of all the men of Judah who come out of their cities. It may be that their supplication will come before the Lord, and that every one will turn from his evil way, for great is the anger and wrath that the Lord has pronounced against this people." And Baruch the son of Neriah did all that Jeremiah the prophet ordered him about reading from the scroll the words of the Lord in the Lord's house. (Jer 36:4-8)

> So they went into the court to the king, having put the scroll in the chamber of Elishama the secretary; and they reported all the words to the king. Then the king sent Jehudi to get the scroll, and he took it from the chamber of Elishama the secretary; and Jehudi read it to the king and all the princes who stood beside the king. It

was the ninth month, and the king was sitting in the winter house and there was a fire burning in the brazier before him. As Jehudi read three or four columns, the king would cut them off with a penknife and throw them into the fire in the brazier, until the entire scroll was consumed in the fire that was in the brazier. Yet neither the king, nor any of his servants who heard all these words, was afraid, nor did they rend their garments. Even when Elnathan and Delaiah and Gemariah urged the king not to burn the scroll, he would not listen to them. (vv.20-25)

Now, after the king had burned the scroll with the words which Baruch wrote at Jeremiah's dictation, the word of the Lord came to Jeremiah: "Take another scroll and write on it all the former words that were in the first scroll, which Jehoiakim the king of Judah has burned." (vv.27-28)

Then Jeremiah took another scroll and gave it to Baruch the scribe, the son of Neriah, who wrote on it at the dictation of Jeremiah all the words of the scroll which Jehoiakim king of Judah had burned in the fire; and many similar words were added to them. (v.32)

I, Paul, write this greeting with my own hand. (1 Cor 16:21)

See with what large letters I am writing to you with my own hand. (Gal 6:11)

I, Paul, write this greeting with my own hand. (Col 4:18a)

I, Paul, write this greeting with my own hand. This is the mark in every letter of mine; it is the way I write. (2 Thess 3:17)

When one takes into consideration that *graphē* (scripture; from the Latin *scriptura*) is from the verb *graphō* (write, inscribe; from the Latin verb *scribo*), then in the Bible what is *written* is equivalent to being *officially written* and thus *scripturalized*. This is evident to someone cognizant of the original Hebrew that lies behind the Greek Septuagint translation. The third part of the Old Testament, which contains books of different literary genres,[6] simply dubbed *ketubim* (Books, Writings), is intented to be read aloud to the hearers, as is reflected in their Greek denomination as *anaginōskomena* (to be read aloud; for reading aloud).

It follows then that the letter to the Hebrews, precisely *as scripture*, is the "word of exhortation" entrusted to the "leaders" of the Pauline churches who are to teach their flocks *out of it*, not *about it*. To underscore this legacy, the author singles out the leaders three times:

> Remember your leaders, those who spoke to you the word of God; consider the outcome of their life, and imitate their faith. Jesus Christ is the same yesterday and today and for ever. Do not be led away by diverse and strange teachings; for it is well that the heart be strengthened by grace, not by foods, which have not benefited their adherents. (Heb 13:7-9)

> Obey your leaders and submit to them; for they are keeping watch over your souls, as men who will have to give account. Let them do this joyfully, and not sadly, for that would be of no advantage to you. (v.17)

> Greet all your leaders and all the saints. (v.24a)

The first passage introduces the leaders as the heirs of Paul who "spoke[7] the word of God" (13:7a). Like Paul they are examples in living as well as teaching (v.7b): "For it has been granted to

---

[6] These include Prayers (Psalms), Wisdom literature (Job, Proverbs, Ecclesiastes), History (Ruth, Esther, Ezra and Nehemiah, 1 and 2 Chronicles), Poems (Song of Songs, Lamentations), Prophecy (Daniel).

[7] The verb used here *elalēsan* is the one found in the Pauline letters in conjunction with "preaching the gospel."

you that for the sake of Christ you should not only believe in him but also suffer for his sake, *engaged in the same conflict which you saw and now hear to be mine*" (Phil 1:29-30); "Brethren, join in imitating me, and mark those who so live as you have an example in us." (3:17) Just as Paul did (Eph 4:20) and scripturalized in his letters, the leaders are to keep teaching Jesus Christ so that throughout the generations of hearers Christ will remain "the same yesterday and today and for ever" (Heb 13:8). In other words, the leaders are to continue teaching this letter and all the Pauline letters *as scripture* without twisting their content as others do (v.9a), as witnessed in 2 Peter: "So also our beloved brother Paul wrote to you according to the wisdom given him, speaking of this as he does in all his letters. There are some things in them hard to understand, which the ignorant and unstable twist to their own destruction, as they do *the other scriptures.*" (3:15b-16) Because of their position, the leaders will have to give account (*logon apodōsantes*; Heb 13:17), as will the Apostle.[8] Finally, the leaders are considered to be in a special category among the "saints" (v.24a) as are the bishops and deacons: "Paul and Timothy, servants of Christ Jesus, to all the saints in Christ Jesus who are at Philippi, with the bishops and deacons" (Phil 1:1). The addressees of Hebrews have been prepared to make this connection since they just heard, in the canonical sequence, the Pastoral Epistles addressed to the bishops Timothy and Titus and the letter to Philemon, the head of his house church and thus de facto its "bishop."

Now that he has secured the legacy based on the scripturalized Pauline message, the author closes his correspondence by reminding his hearers of the coming of the Lord, when not only

---

[8] See above my comments on 4:12-13 and 5:11-13 on pp 65 and 87.

the leaders but the Apostle himself will have to give account. "*All the saints*" (Heb 13:24) will have to answer as to whether or not they will have lived their lives according to God's will: "Now may the God of peace who brought again from the dead our Lord Jesus, the great shepherd of the sheep, by the blood of the eternal covenant, equip you with everything good that you may do his will, working in you that which is pleasing in his sight, through Jesus Christ; to whom be glory for ever and ever. Amen." (vv.20-21) The phraseology of this hope is copied from Ezekiel:

> I will save my flock, they shall no longer be a prey; and I will judge between sheep and sheep. And I will set up over them one shepherd, my servant David, and he shall feed them: he shall feed them and be their *shepherd*. And I, the Lord, will be their God, and my servant David shall be prince among them; I, the Lord, have spoken. I will make with them a *covenant* of *peace*. (34:22-25a)

> My servant David shall be king over them; and they shall all have one *shepherd*. *They shall follow my ordinances and be careful to observe my statutes* ... I will make a *covenant* of *peace* with them; it shall be an everlasting covenant with them; and I will bless them and multiply them, and will set my sanctuary in the midst of them for evermore. My dwelling place shall be with them; and I will be their God, and they shall be my people. (37:24, 26-27)

When one hears the closing remarks of the letter metaphorically, the picture that emerges is that Paul is already deceased and so is Timothy, his main adjutant. The end result is that the "saints" are left in the care of the "leaders" who will hopefully "keep watch over" them (Heb 13:17) according to the Pauline teaching scripturalized in this letter and, by extension, the entire Pauline corpus since Hebrews is the last "word" in that corpus. This scripturalized relationship between "leaders" and "saints" should follow the pattern delineated in vv.5-7: both the divine statement to watch over his people and their obedient response to him are "worded" out of scripture and will remain until the "close of the age" (Mt 28:20) after Jesus has ascended to be "seated at the right hand of the throne of God" (Heb 12:2), and also after Paul and Timothy have ended their days on earth. However, since Paul taught in 1 Corinthians 15 and 1 Thessalonians 4 that the dead in Christ shall return with the Lord, Paul's hope is that not only he will be "restored" to them "soon" (*takhion*; the sooner, Heb 13:19), but that Timothy, who "has been released" (*apolelymenon*) *from this life through his death*,[9] will also join Paul, and they both will *come* "with the Lord" (1 Thess 4:17) to see them "soon" (*takhion*; Heb 13:23). These verses contain the only instances in this letter of the root *takh*— that often occurs in conjunction with the "coming" of the Lord.[10]

The reference to Italy, a rarity in scripture,[11] is intended to give the impression that the letter was written from Rome, just as the reference to Phoebe and Cenchreae in Romans 16:1 gives the impression that that letter was written from the Eastern parts of the empire.[12] By having these two letters (Romans and Hebrews) bracket the Pauline corpus, the Pauline school, which is behind the canon as well as the content of the New Testament, wanted to impress on the hearers that Paul's gospel message has spread over all of the Roman empire, and that whether the letter comes

---

[9] This is one of the meanings the verb *apolyomai* carries, as is clear from Lk 2:29: "Lord, now *lettest thou thy servant depart* (*apolyeis*) in peace, according to thy word."
[10] See Rev 2:16; 3:11; 22:7, 12, 20.
[11] It is found only thrice more in Acts (18:2; 27:1, 6).
[12] Phoebe is a unique instance and Cenchreae, the port of Corinth, occurs only once more at Acts 18:18. See my comments on this matter in *C-Rom* 270-2.

from the East or from the West, "(the) Jesus Christ (that Paul preached)[13] is (now) the same yesterday and today and for ever" (Heb 13:8) and the "believers," Jew and Gentile alike, are part of the same "olive tree" (Rom 11:13-24). Even if the Romans never get to see Paul (Rom 15:22-29) and even if the recipients of the letter to the Hebrews do not hear his name mentioned in the letter, his visual "absence" is "filled" by the presence of Timothy (Rom 16:21; Heb 13:23) of whom he wrote:

> I hope in the Lord Jesus to *send* Timothy to you soon (*takheōs*), so that I may be cheered by news of you. *I have no one like him*, who will be genuinely anxious for your welfare. They all look after their own interests, not those of Jesus Christ. But Timothy's worth you know, how as *a son with a father he has served with me in the gospel.* I hope therefore to send him just as soon as I see how it will go with me; and I trust in the Lord that shortly (*takheōs*) I myself shall *come also.* (Phil 2:19-24)

By the time the letter to the Hebrews reaches the hearers' ears, the value of Timothy as the recipient of Paul's "testament" (2 Tim) will be sealed, which in turn explains Paul's "absence" in Hebrews.

In closing, the author ends with the usual greetings (Heb 13:24) and with the wish that divine "grace" would abide with the recipients (v.25), both typical of all Pauline correspondence.

---

[13] See 2 Cor: "For if some one comes and preaches another Jesus than the one we preached, or if you receive a different spirit from the one you received, or if you accept a different gospel from the one you accepted, you submit to it readily enough ... And what I do I will continue to do, in order to undermine the claim of those who would like to claim that in their boasted mission they work on the same terms as we do. For such men are false apostles, deceitful workmen, disguising themselves as apostles of Christ. And no wonder, for even Satan disguises himself as an angel of light. So it is not strange if his servants also disguise themselves as servants of righteousness. Their end will correspond to their deeds." (11:3-4, 12-15)

Further Reading

Commentaries and Studies

Gordon, R. P. *Hebrews*. Readings: A New Biblical Commentary. (2nd ed.) Sheffield, UK: Sheffield, Phoenix, 2008.

Grelot, P. *Une lecture de l'épître aux Hébreux*. Lire la Bible 132. Paris: Cerf, 2003.

Harrington, D. J. *What Are They Saying About The Letter to the Hebrews?* New York—Mahwah, NJ: Paulist, 2005.

Harrington, D. J. *The Letter to the Hebrews*. New Collegeville Bible Commentary 11. Collegeville, MN: Liturgical Press, 2006.

Johnson, E. S. *Hebrews*. Interpretation Bible Studies. Louisville, KY—London: Westminster John Knox, 2008.

Johnson, L. T. *Hebrews. A Commentary*. New Testament Library. Louisville, KY—London: Westminster John Knox, 2006.

Koester, C. R. *Hebrews. A New Translation with Introduction and Commentary*. Anchor Bible 36. New York—London: Doubleday, 2001.

Mitchell, A. C. *Hebrews*. Sacra Pagina 13. Collegeville, MN: Liturgical Press, 2007.

Stedman, R. C. *Hebrews*. IVP New Testament Commentary 15. Downers Grove, IL: IVP Academic, 2010.

Vanhoye, A. *La Lettre aux Hébreux. Jésus-Christ, médiateur d'une nouvelle alliance.* Jésus et Jésus-Christ 84. Paris: Desclée, 2001.

Wright, N. T. *Hebrews for Everyone*. Louisville, KY: Westminster John Knox, 2004.

Articles

Gleason, R. C. "The Old Testament Background of Rest in Hebrews 3:7-4:11." *Bibliotheca Sacra* 157 (627, '00) 281-303.

Granerød, G. "Melchizedek in Hebrews 7." *Biblica* 90 (2, '09) 188-202.

Gray, P. "Brotherly Love and the High Priest Christology of Hebrews." *Journal of Biblical Literature* 122 (2, 03) 335-51.

Jipp, J. W. "The Son's Entrance into the Heavenly World: The Soteriological Necessity of the Scriptural Catena in Hebrews 1.5-14." *New Testament Studies* 56 (4, '10) 557-75.

Johnson, L. T. "The Scriptural World of Hebrews." *Interpretation* 57 (3, 03) 237-50.

Koester, C. R. "Hebrews, Rhetoric, and the Future of Humanity." *Catholic Biblical Quarterly* 64 (1, 02) 103-23.

Leithart, P. J. "Womb of the World: Baptism and the Priesthood of the New Covenant in Hebrews 10.09-22." *Journal for the Study of the New Testament* 78 ('00) 49-65.

Mackie, S. D. "Confession of the Son of God in the Exordium of Hebrews." *Journal for the Study of the New Testament* 30 (4, '08) 437-53.

Omar, O. R. "Embracing the 'Other' as an Extension of the Self: Muslim Reflections on the Epistle to the Hebrews 13:2." *Anglican Theological Review* 91 (3, '09) 433-41.

Perry, P. S. "Making Fear Personal: Hebrews 5.11-6.12 and the Argument from Shame." *Journal for the Study of the New Testament* 32 (1, '09) 261-279.

Rooke, D.W. "Jesus as Royal Priest: Reflections on the Interpretation of the Melchizedek Tradition in Heb 7." *Biblica* 81 (1, '00) 81-94.

Smillie, G.R. "'ὁ λόγος τοῦ Θεοῦ' in Hebrews 4:12-13." *Novum Testamentum* 46 (4, 04) 338-59.

Smillie, G.R. "'The other λόγος' at the End of Heb. 4:13." *Novum Testamentum* 47 (1, 05) 19-25.

Still, T. D. "*Christos* as *Pistos*: The Faith(fullness) of Jesus in the Epistle to the Hebrews." *Catholic Biblical Quarterly* 69 (4, 07) 746-55.

Swetnam, S. "Ἐξ ἑνός in Hebrews 2,11." *Biblica* 88 (4, 07) 517-25.

Swetnam, S. "ὁ ἀπόστολος in Hebrews 3,1." *Biblica* 89 (2, '08) 252-62.

Thiessen, M. "Hebrews and the end of Exodus." *Scandinavian Novum Testamentum* 49 (4, 07) 353-69.

www.ingramcontent.com/pod-product-compliance
Lightning Source LLC
Chambersburg PA
CBHW060536100426
42743CB00009B/1546